Giving Your Customers The Royal Treatment

Treat Clients The Right Way So They Become Lifetime Raving Fans

By
Marc Poulos

Copyright © 2013 www.MarcPoulosPainting.com

Published by Nomad CEO Publishing

ISBN-13:978-1493626908

ISBN-10:1493626906

Legal Description

All Rights Reserved. No part of this publication may be reproduced in any form or by any means, including scanning, photocopying, or otherwise without prior written permission of the copyright holder.

Disclaimer and Terms of Use: The Author and Publisher has strived to be as accurate and complete as possible in the creation of this book, notwithstanding the fact that he does not warrant or represent at any time that the contents within are accurate due to the rapidly changing nature of the Internet. While all attempts have been made to verify information provided in this publication, the Author and Publisher assumes no responsibility for errors, omissions, or contrary interpretation of the subject matter herein. Any perceived slights of specific persons, peoples, or organizations are unintentional. In practical advice books, like anything else in life, there are no guarantees of income made. Readers are cautioned to rely on their own judgment about their individual circumstances to act accordingly. This book is not intended for use as a source of legal, business, accounting or financial advice. All readers are advised to seek services of competent professionals in the legal, business, accounting, and finance fields.

Introduction

Brick and mortar businesses have been around since the beginning of time. The ancient Romans would set up their "stores" in the marketplace, and sell their wares. Word of mouth was the only way to let others know what they had to sell.

Today, the internet has not only opened up a whole new world for brick and mortar businesses, but for very successful online businesses. Gone are the days of spending a fortune in Yellow Page ads, or going door-to-door placing coupons in mailboxes.

There is finesse today about how we let others know who we are, where we are and what we are. There are a billion and one new marketing techniques coming to light daily, and if we're not on that bandwagon already, we need to be.

Finding the "expert" in a niche has never been easier for the customer or client. There was a time when being the best in your neighborhood, city or region was more than enough to ensure your success.

But the internet has changed all that. It's now very easy for prospective clients to click a button and find out who the best experts in the world are for the topic or niche they are searching for.

Your customers will search for the very best product that will fulfill their wants and needs, delivered by the top expert they can find and afford.

So to win in today's business world, you must help your clients to determine that your solution is what they need, and that you are the best person for them to get it from.

That is why having a complete platform is so critical to your success.

I wrote this book to help you accelerate your business growth by learning what is working today to build and sustain a successful business.

Nothing you will find here is ivory-tower, pie-in-the-sky or business-school nonsense. Everything you will learn is from the real live in-the-trenches experience of someone who puts my pants on one leg at a time, invests my own time and hard-earned dollars into building my business, has gone through the ups and downs of running a small business during the deepest recession in our nation's history and has experienced tremendous, real world success.

So relax, open your mind, and breathe in the knowledge and expertise of what has worked, what keeps working and what will continue to work to transform not only my business, but the lives of my clients and their families as well.

And if you get even just one good idea from this book and take action to put it to use, then I'll have accomplished my goal of helping to transform the life of one more of my fellow small business owners.

To Your Future Success,

Marc Poulos

Table of Contents

Introduction iii

Chapter 1: Marc Poulos
Giving Your Customers The Royal Treatment 1

Chapter 2: Steve Sipress
The 5 Essential Keys To Successful Small
Business Marketing 9

Chapter 3: Phil Brakefield
A Promotional Products Primer…For Hardware Stores…Cost-Effective Ways to Keep Your Name Front and Center with Your Customers! 21

Chapter 4: Mary Forte
Why Your Marketing Should Be As Unique As Your
Business 29

Chapter 5: Jon Bockman
Leader Of The Pack 39

Chapter 6: Russell Burck
Live the Life of Your Dreams After You're 65: Three Big Mistakes that Retiring Professionals Make that Keep them Wondering What They'll Do next and Whether They'll Be Bored in Retirement 51

Chapter 7: Bryan Regnier
Pain Management for Business Success 63

Chapter 8: Craig Leach
AACCELing At Your Business 75

Chapter 9: John Senska
How To Safeguard Your Clients Against The Unethical Competitor Out To Steal Their Money 91

Chapter 10: Robert Bilger
To Err Is Human; To Really Mess Things Up Takes
A Computer! 99

Chapter 11: Ronald Guzik
5 Secrets to Being Super Productive, Implementing More of
Your Ideas, And Building Your Business Faster 107

Chapter 12: Jerry "Ace" Luciano
Success "Secrets" for Sales and Business 121

Chapter 13: Greg Bowen
The Ultimate Guide To Mold Removal 137

Chapter 14: Christine Howatt
4 Simple Strategies That Will Make Your Business Stand Out
From the Crowd (or from your Competition) 151

Chapter 15: Phil Brakefield
Winners: Hardware Store Promotional Products
that WORK! 161

Chapter 1

Giving Your Customers The Royal Treatment

By Marc Poulos

Are your customers just cash cows, or are they people that you would like to work with over and over again? Do they have respect for the work you do, or is it get in, get the job done, and get out?

You may be the owner of your company, but I am going to show you how you can become the "King" or "Queen," just by Giving Your Customers The Royal Treatment.

I started painting homes during summer vacations while attending college. After college, I had a brief career in the real estate and financial services field. As good a job as that was, I realized that my passion was in beautifying homes. I enjoyed painting during my summers, and I was always very proud when the job was done. Not only could I see the results of my handiwork, but I also saw the joy in the faces of my customers. And that was worth the late days, the sweat-filled t-shirts, and the sore arms.

Since I now knew what I wanted to be when I grew up, I began working with a variety of small craftsman shops, just to get some more experience under my belt, and also to get my foot in the door.

I truly believe that my idea of how a business should be run came when I started serving an apprenticeship with the Ritz-Carlton Hotel in Chicago. If you've ever been to a Ritz-Carlton, you know that they are well-known for their customer service. If you are walking down the hall and need help, it doesn't matter

GIVING YOUR CUSTOMERS THE ROYAL TREATMENT

if it is a maid, an employee on break, or the manager on duty, they will stop what they are doing and personally take care of your needs. They really have it all together with their customer service.

Eventually I spent seven years beautifying the Ritz-Carlton, and my commitment to excellence won me the distinguished honor of "Top Apprentice" from Washburne Trade School in Chicago—one of the premier schools of its kind in the country.

In 1996 I left the Ritz and formed my own company, MVP Decorating. In 2009 I guess I got my "Aha Moment," and decided to return to the personal touch of the early years and the unparalleled service of the days at the Ritz-Carlton. I made a few business changes and formed Marc Poulos Painting and Decorating, where I knew that my name and reputation would be on every job, and on the line.

My goal was to constantly raise the bar of quality craftsmanship and client service in the painting and decorating business. In so doing I hoped to create lifetime relationships with loyal clients who continually referred us to family, friends and associates. Through hard work, trial and error, and keeping my ears and eyes open I was able to transform a usually disruptive service into a pleasure.

Doing the Right Thing

In order to be able to give that personalized service, I had to think of every job that I stepped into as if I were doing it for my mom or grandmother. If my grandma asked me to change the paint color at the last minute, could I tell her "no?" I don't think so. If she asked me to paint another room, could I tell her I didn't have the time? If I knew what was good for me, I would keep my mouth shut and just smile.

Now don't get me wrong. I am not a total soft touch. After all, business is business. But, if a customer has a special request, I will do everything in my power to fulfill their wish. After all, you do catch a lot more flies with honey than vinegar.

We have learned over the years that it's the little things that make the customers happy and satisfied…..enough to have you back later for more work, or just referring you to their friends or family.

Let's take a look at some of the things we stand behind when we want to treat our customers like royalty:

- If we are 15 minutes late, the customer does not pay for that day
- We try our best to leave the house as clean, or cleaner, than when we showed up. If for some reason we have an accident and make a mess, either we clean it up ourselves, or we will pay to have a professional cleaner come in
- Yes, we do windows. Whether we are painting window sills inside or out, we always finish the job with making sure that windows are the cleanest possible
- If we track dirt in , it's cleaned up immediately
- We do our best to anticipate the needs of our clients
- We try to gear our service to each client
- If a client needs another service provider, like an electrician, we will do the research and give them recommendations
- We do background checks on each person we hire, and give a record of our workers on the job to our clients so

GIVING YOUR CUSTOMERS THE ROYAL TREATMENT

they know that whoever is in their house is trustworthy
- We always leave a gift for our clients, whether it be a plant or flowers or cookies, after their job is done
- We send a survey to each customer upon the completion of a job. If a customer has even the tiniest negative feedback, we contact them and immediately find out how we could improve in that area
- Each customer receives not only a personalized Christmas card from us, but also a birthday card. It is so easy to get this information on Facebook or researching on Google
- We go out of our way to give 1000%

Just like with the Ritz-Carlton, we pride ourselves not only on the work that we do, but more importantly, on our customer service. And just like with the Ritz, my workers also have permission to take care of a client's request (within reason, of course).

I have many customers that will ask us about our referral system. For a moment they are shocked when I tell them that we don't have one. Then they light up when we tell them that we have a "Pay It Forward System" instead. When they recommend my company to someone else, we allow that person to "test drive" us for a day. All they need to do is to buy is the paint. Our labor is free. If we get done with the job in 8 hours and shake hands and go our separate ways, no hard feelings.

But more often than not, we will get a call back from that customer. It could be six weeks or six months down the road, but they remembered what we had done for them and how we treated them, and now they need our services for a larger job, which could run anywhere from $4,000 to $10,000. Not too shabby for a free day of work.

The Flip Side

We have our positive rules down, but what about the other side? Are there things NOT to do when you are at a client's house? Of course there are! Let's take a look at a few things that should not be done:

- All of my workers look professional. No one works in torn jeans or a t-shirt with profanity on it, or a shirt that hasn't been washed in a week.
- We don't go in dirty. We dress to impress.
- There is no smoking on or near the property. If a worker does have a cigarette during lunch, then they had better use gum or breath mints and Febreeze before they walk back into the house.
- Absolutely no profanity in a client's house.
- Never talk down to a client.
- Unless something could harm our client, the workers, or is illegal, "No" is not in our vocabulary.
- If we see a problem, like a live wire, we will contact our electrician to come down and get it repaired as quickly as possible.
- Don't nickel and dime your client. Give them some freebies. You'll be paid back tenfold later on.
- Be careful of the client's personal belongings. You break it, you bought it.
- Never, ever go snooping in a client's house. Unless they allow you to use their bathroom, you should never leave the room you are working in.

So there you have it. It takes very little to make a client happy, but it takes a little more to keep them happy and coming back for more.

GIVING YOUR CUSTOMERS THE ROYAL TREATMENT

Build *relationships* with your clients, because once they are formed, the profits will follow.

MARC POULOS

About Marc Poulos

Marc Poulos started painting homes during summer vacations while attending college. After he finished college, Marc had a brief career in the real estate and financial services field. He then realized that his passion was beautifying homes.

Marc began working with a variety of small craftsman shops, before serving an apprenticeship with the Ritz-Carlton Hotel in Chicago. His commitment to excellence won him the distinguished honor of "Top Apprentice" from Washburne Trade School in Chicago—one of the premier schools of its kind in the country.

Marc spent seven years beautifying the Ritz-Carlton. He then formed MVP Decorating, which was in existence from 1996-2009. Wanting to return to the personal touch of the early years and the unparalleled service of the days at the Ritz-Carlton, Marc made a few business changes and formed Marc Poulos Painting and Decorating, where he knew his name and reputation would be on every job.

Marc's mission is to deliver an unparalleled experience by being the best painter in the industry. As a result, his company

GIVING YOUR CUSTOMERS THE ROYAL TREATMENT

continues to grow and prosper from the referrals of his raving fans who share their experiences with friends, family and associates.

The Chicago Tribune raves simply, "Marc Poulos, Painter Extraordinaire."

Bonus Offer

As a Bonus to you for reading this book, Marc Poulos Painting will give you a

Free Painter For A Day!

You will have your own painting expert at your disposal for eight full hours. He will show up with a fully-stocked truck to complete any job you want. You just purchase the paint and let him know what you want done. This can include painting one or more rooms, doing minor touch-ups, minor wall and/or ceiling repair, painting of trim – virtually anything you want in one full eight-hour day!

Geographic restrictions apply, and this offer is subject to availability. To find out if you qualify for your own *Free Painter For A Day,* **call**

847-483-9094

Chapter 2

The 5 Essential Keys To Successful Small Business Marketing

By Steve Sipress

An all-too-common, critical mistake that most small-business owners make (I've owned dozens of my own businesses, and I have to admit that very early in my career I made this mistake myself) is that they fail to make the critical transition that all successful business owners must make to create wealth and thrive, especially during this challenging economy: Moving from DOER to MARKETER.

When it comes right down to it, there are really only three areas of any business:

- Generating leads (marketing)
- Converting leads into customers/clients/patients (sales)
- Fulfilling the promise of the sale (the "doing" of the business)

In my 30-plus years of consulting to thousands of business owners, the overwhelming majority of them tend to hide out in this third area of their business, concentrating almost all of their time, effort and resources on the "doing" of their business. If you ask them what they do, they'll define themselves in exactly that way ("I'm a dentist," "I'm a plumber," "I'm a lawyer," etc.).

It's not their fault. That's how we've all been taught to think.

But it's a recipe for frustration, overwork and under-enjoyment of small-business ownership, and often for the failure of the business.

GIVING YOUR CUSTOMERS THE ROYAL TREATMENT

If you want to become a wealthy and successful small-business owner, you MUST concentrate the majority of your time, energy and money on becoming a better marketer of your business. You must make this quantum leap to becoming "a marketer of dental services," "a marketer of plumbing services," "a marketer of legal services," etc.

Now I'm not telling you not to keep up with the latest tools and techniques in the "doing" of your business. Definitely keep doing that. But let's face it: You're not going to double your income over the next twelve months by getting twice as good at the "doing" of your business — but you may very well do so if you get twice as good at marketing your business.

Here are The 5 Essential Keys To Successful Small Business Marketing:

1. Define Your Unique Selling Proposition ("USP")
2. Create An Effective, "Irresistible" Sales Offer
3. Avoid Common Marketing Pitfalls
4. Develop And Use A Smart Marketing Perspective
5. Get Results!

I'll guide you through each one of these so that you can see exactly how to use them to catapult your business to greater heights than ever before…

I. Define Your Unique Selling Proposition ("USP")

Coming up with an effective USP for your business that sets you apart from all of your competition and makes you The Obvious Choice to do business with, can be a challenging, time-consuming, painstaking task.

But I am a firm believer that this will be the best investment of your time and effort as a small business owner, because once you have created your own "Killer USP," you will have raised yourself and your business up out of the endless sea of "me-too" small businesses who provide the same products or services that you do by setting yourself apart in the eyes of your prospects, practically compelling them to do business with you.

A lot goes into creating an effective USP. I teach entire workshops on the subject, and I've helped create them for hundreds of business owners. But here's a quick summary of the process you can use to create your own Killer USP...

1. Take the time to ask yourself some questions *from the perspective of your prospects and customers, clients or patients:*

    - What frustrates you about other businesses in your industry?
    - What would it take for someone to get *your* attention?
    - What needs do *you* have that need to be met?
    - What are the promises *you* want fulfilled?

2. Once you figure out the answers to these questions, you can start putting together a plan to cure those frustrations, solve those problems and meet those needs.

3. Then take a look at what USP's your competitors are using to help you discover the "opportunity gaps" between what your prospects want and what they're being offered. Your USP should fill one or more of those "gaps" so that you set yourself apart from your

GIVING YOUR CUSTOMERS THE ROYAL TREATMENT

competition and make yourself The Obvious Choice for people to do business with.

Remember: your USP is what you are "promising" your customers, clients or patients, so make sure you can deliver – or even better, over-deliver.

II. Create An Effective, "Irresistible" Sales Offer

To develop an effective sales plan, you need to:

1. Come up with a headline that will grab the immediate attention of your audience.
2. Share the benefits of your products and services – thinking about your customers' perspective instead of yours.
3. Identify the specific needs your products and services meet.
4. Make it easy to do business with you by offering strong guarantees.
5. Share your specific, Unique Sales Proposition.
6. Make it crystal clear to your customers, clients or patients exactly how they should respond and act.
7. Motivate your ideal prospects with a strong, compelling call to action.

Here's the bottom line...

You need to explain what makes your products and services special, and compel people to buy from you. If they don't feel like they NEED your product or service, they won't buy. You need to answer a question, solve a problem or feed an obsession that they have.

Finally, you need to provide them with all the information they need to make an informed and confident decision. Buyer's remorse is one of the worst things that can happen for any business owner, and there are definite steps smart marketers take to avoid it.

III. Avoid Common Marketing Pitfalls

There are 5 Major Marketing Pitfalls that many businesses fall into which you need to avoid:

1. Ignoring market testing and pushing on with an inaccurate plan.
2. Offering an incomplete case, or reasons, throughout their marketing plan.
3. Failing to notice and figure out the true needs of their prospective customers, clients or patients.
4. Failing to diversify their marketing options.
5. Failing to get market opinions on their offers.

These are all areas to avoid. If you work through the lessons I teach at **SSSMarketingUniversity.com,** avoiding these pitfalls will become easy and natural.

IV. Develop and Use A Smart Marketing Perspective

Having a smart marketing perspective is important, especially if you want to absolutely crush any or all of your competition and become The Obvious Choice in your chosen marketplace. You can do this through a number of different techniques and activities:

1. Keep a marketing journal and write down anything

GIVING YOUR CUSTOMERS THE ROYAL TREATMENT

innovative you see being used – regardless of the industry. Often the answers to your marketing challenges are found by looking *outside* your particular industry. Most small business owners have such a narrow focus that they never examine or study marketing being used by anyone who isn't a direct competitor. You can set yourself apart by being the only one in your industry to use a strategy or tactic from a different industry – likely something your competitors aren't even aware of and will be clueless to overcome.

2. Keep encouraging your marketing department (and yourself) to try new things and dump the ones that aren't working.

3. Periodically "mystery shop" your own company by ordering under a different name so you can analyze the process of ordering, shipping, online store, customer service and your product or service itself. This will show you where the areas for improvement are in the customer experience you're currently providing.

4. Become a student of advertising by reading every ad you can find (I get the funniest looks from people in waiting rooms as I skip all the magazine articles to read just the ads!); and keep the good ones you find in your own "swipe file" to give you ideas to consider for your own future ads.

5. Whenever you're in a store or a mall, observe how consumers behave in different situations and how they consider their purchases.

6. Step down a notch or two and work on the front lines – in person or on the phones – with your sales and customer service staff.

7. Continuously acknowledge and thank your staff, vendors and customers. Everyone works and shops better when they feel appreciated.

8. Always gather and listen to feedback from employees and customers.

9. Continuously test markets, ads, and marketing strategies and techniques. This is the only way to stay successful by cutting wasteful spending and knowing what's working – and, more importantly, what's not.

10. Offer more and more valuable information in your marketing than anyone else. The more information you offer, the more products and services you'll sell.

11. A great marketing plan can only get better. Continue to fine tune and refine your marketing plan based on testing results and feedback.

12. Be aware of the image your company is conveying through your marketing. Do your prospects and customers, clients or patients feel you really care about them, or that you're just trying to take their money?

13. Improve your best marketing areas, and drop those that aren't working.

14. Focus on what you say, and how you say it. The best marketing ideas naturally turn into the best marketing.

15. Develop all your ads, campaigns and sales materials to create and share compelling, relevant and factual information.

16. Make sure you work with a skilled, experienced Business Coach – one who is an expert in Direct Response Marketing and has gotten dramatic RESULTS for many

GIVING YOUR CUSTOMERS THE ROYAL TREATMENT

clients in various industries. All top performers have coaches!

By using these techniques and more that I teach, you can make yourself The Obvious Choice for your ideal prospects.

V. Get Results!

The last area I'll talk about is creating satisfied customers. If your customers aren't satisfied, you've wasted all your marketing resources and all chance of positive word-of-mouth advertising and repeat business. You can satisfy your customers by:

1. Providing quality products and services
2. Providing high-quality customer service
3. Providing a low-pressure, highly-informative sales experience
4. Taking all the risk away with a great guarantee

I'll assume that you've got the first couple of these covered. You really shouldn't even be in business in the first place if you don't believe that what you're selling is something of value, and you don't genuinely want to help people. This is also of critical importance if you want to get the most out of the strategies I teach.

Will the marketing strategies and tactics I teach help even small business owners who insist on providing low-quality products and services? Of course they will. But common sense tells you that even the very best referral and repeat business strategies won't work nearly as well for businesses whose offerings are inferior.

As for numbers 3 and 4 on this list, those are topics for in-depth discussion and training all by themselves. I cover the specific steps involved to do both as a part of the 150+ hours of video curriculum at **SSSMarketingUniversity.com.**

Is this a lot to learn and implement? Sure it is. That's why the sharp small business owners who focus their time and energy in these areas are reaping huge benefits – even while the vast majority of small businesses are suffering in this difficult economy.

If you're ready to stop being a part of the frustrated, confused and under-performing majority of small business owners and start transforming your business into a customer-getting, wealth-producing machine, then you'll make the quantum leap from being just a "doer" of your business to a "marketer" of your business.

And you'll focus most of your time, attention and resources on getting pretty darn good at it – including working with the very best coaches and service providers.

By doing this you'll experience a massive transformation in your income and lifestyle, and will join the Top 4% of business owners who use their businesses to create wealth and freedom for them and their families.

After all, isn't that why you started your business in the first place?

GIVING YOUR CUSTOMERS THE ROYAL TREATMENT

About Steve Sipress

If you want to grow your business slowly – or just maintain it as it is, you'll have to do that all on your own.

But if you want dramatic growth in your income and lifestyle, then Steve's out-of-the-box, time-tested strategies and tactics could be the keys to your dreams.

You can benefit from Steve's coaching experience and expertise to revolutionize your business – yes, even in this challenging economy – at one of the many in-person entrepreneur events he hosts, OR from the comfort of your own home anywhere in the world.

You can also learn basic and advanced direct response marketing strategies and tactics from 150+ hours of video instruction, plus use any or all of Steve's multi-million-dollar, proven "done-for-you" marketing materials at **SSSMarketingUniversity.com.** That website has been called The Single Most Powerful Client Attraction Program Available Anywhere, and you could be using it to skyrocket your income anytime you want, 24/7, along with hundreds of other sharp, successful business leaders.

As a bonus for you because you are reading this book, Steve has arranged for you to discover for yourself exactly how **SSSMarketingUniversity.com** will help you build a market-dominating business by giving you a Free Trial offer:

Free Trial Offer

To take advantage of this Bonus, go to:

www.SSSMarketingUniversity.com/bookbonus

Steve is a successful and award-winning serial entrepreneur, who has created and built nearly a dozen successful companies of his own, and he can help you do the same – more quickly and easily than you've ever imagined. In fact, you can immediately use plenty of his simple and powerful strategies and tactics that work especially well in this currently frustrating economy!

Steve is a celebrated author, speaker and business coach who has established profitable businesses and helped thousands of ambitious and aggressive business owners, entrepreneurs, executives and sales professionals all around the world. He has written numerous newsletters and articles on sales and marketing for a wide range of publications and has appeared on radio and television, helping millions of people along the way.

If you want the very best, hard-hitting, no-nonsense caring advice and help you can get, then "Straight-Talk Steve" could be exactly what you and your business need most.

GIVING YOUR CUSTOMERS THE ROYAL TREATMENT

If you're in the Midwest, you can meet other like-minded business people in person and learn from the world's leading entrepreneur experts at one of Steve's many "Chicagoland's Sharpest Entrepreneurs" live events that he's hosted since September 2008.

You also have the chance to work with other entrepreneurs, business owners, executives and professionals like yourself – like the other authors of this book – who want to learn better, more effective ways to market their businesses and grow their incomes, thanks to Steve's online group and individual coaching programs.

Whether you're a current or future business superstar, Steve can help you get exactly where you want to go as quickly, easily and powerfully as YOU want – with massive results, both short-term and long-term.

www.SteveSipress.com
www.SSSMarketingUniversity.com/bookbonus
www.LinkedIn.com/in/SteveSipress
www.Facebook.com/SmallBizHelp
www.Twitter.com/SteveSipress

Chapter 3

A Promotional Products Primer...
For Hardware Stores...

Cost-Effective Ways to Keep Your Name Front and Center with Your Customers!

By Phil Brakefield

The retail hardware business these days is a 24/7 pitch battle.

Chaos, shotgun approach to advertising and a lack of brand clarity are the order of the day.

The big boxes, plus everything from grocery stores to mini-marts to gas stations to dollar stores now offering hardware; market segmentation; erosion of traditional advertising media effectiveness...even missteps at the corporate level...are all contributing to massive challenges for the local hardware store owner to carve out and protect his/her name recognition with customers and prospects.

The predominant strategy du jour seems to be simply to price cut or discount. BOGO is pushed from on high as the way to build customer counts, but there is strong evidence that to stay in business and prosper it would be a good idea not to give stuff away...especially top quality products!

So the obvious question is...how can an individual hardware store owner cost-effectively stay top of mind with customers and prospects without giving away the farm?

The hard truth is, there are no easy answers.

However, there are some really **smart** ones.

GIVING YOUR CUSTOMERS THE ROYAL TREATMENT

Magic pills and cure-all elixirs had a pretty good run back around the turn of the century…but unfortunately we're talking about the LAST century.

But the good news is that there are literally tens of thousands of long-proven, cost-effective, laser-targeted and response-boosting items available that can do wonders for branding your business.

Coupled with your other marketing and advertising spends, these items will ensure that your store will be 'top of mind' with your customers when the need for hardware arises. And the great news is that it costs you next to nothing to have them think of you as "my" hardware store, not "the" hardware store.

Before we go any deeper, let me emphasize that marketing these days is an "AND" world. The question should never be which media you should use to promote your business:

> Circulars? Video? Newsletter? Postcards? Cable? Podcast? Social Media? In-store events? Local sports team sponsorships? Local charity tie-ins? Promotional Products?

The answer is YES to as many of those choices as possible.

Just insert an "AND" in place of the question marks above!

Obviously budgets are ALWAYS the drivers of your marketing/advertising initiatives, but by choosing your media wisely, and perhaps re-thinking what you've always done, a lot of dollars can be freed up to build your brand presence in your market area, and put you way out in front of the competition.

There are some impressive reasons the use of promotional

products should be a major component of your marketing mix.

The numbers below are verified by PPAI (Promotional Products Association International), in annual studies conducted by leading research universities which collect and distill massive volumes of sales data from thousands of promotional products distributors all over the world.

Here's a summary sampling of what the most important 2012 results show that hold great significance to a local, independent hardware store.

This study is entitled, "The Influence of Promotional Products on Consumer Behavior".

1. Seven in 10 consumers recall receiving at least one promotional product in the past 12 months. A similar finding was observed in previous studies. Among those who recalled receiving promotional products, 70% recalled receiving two or more items.

2. Recall of the advertiser and message behind the first promotional item recalled are very high. **_While 88% recalled the advertiser from a promotional product received in the past 12 months_**, **_only 71% recalled advertisers on a newspaper or magazine read a week before, which speaks to the long term power of promotional products to support brand recall._**

3. Retailers are among the most commonly recalled users of promotional products (joining financial services and electronics manufacturers).

4. Eight in ten consumers own between one and 10

GIVING YOUR CUSTOMERS THE ROYAL TREATMENT

promotional products, six in 10 keep them for up to two years, and about half (53%) use a promo item at least once a week, or more often.

5. The main reason for keeping a promotional product is **usefulness.**

6. When it comes to frequency of use, Calendars/Planners (85%), Computer Products (85%) and Electronic Devices and Accessories (82%) take the top three spots.

7. Most promotional products are kept at home (54%) or on the person (24%).

8. Before receiving a promotional product, about half the consumers had done business with the advertiser (55%). After receiving the promotional products, 85% did business with the advertiser.

9. Advertisers were able to increase their business, even among those who hadn't done any business with them before (11%).

What all this means is that it is undeniable that promotional products have a positive impact on consumer attitudes and behavior. The use of promotional products can be linked directly to customer acquisition and retention, and advertisers should use the medium in a strategic way to reinforce customer loyalty and create positive brand (store) awareness.

There are a few other statistics a hardware store owner should be aware of when formulating marketing budgets, and CPI (Cost Per Impression) is paramount among them.

The CPI index speaks directly to ensuring your marketing budget is being formulated and executed in the absolute most cost-effective manner.

Here's a breakdown by traditional media category:

- Radio = .058 per impression
- Magazine = .045 per impression
- Newspaper = .029 per impression
- Television = .018 per impression
- Promotional Products = .004 per impression

The CPI for Promotional Products runs off and leaves the other categories in terms of pure cost effectiveness.

But the REAL opportunity for a local, independent hardware store is to turn that individual CPI into something spectacular and memorable by selecting an item custom-tailored to the recipient, and then using the store history, standing in the community or other notable achievement to create the message/graphic that decorates the item.

The rule of thumb in creating your promotional product selection(s) should be to talk about YOUR store, and its story, in a way that resonates with your local market trading area and segmented customer list.

Co-op affiliations are for the most part a good thing, rife with benefits and efficiencies, but where the rubber meets the road, i.e., getting customers through the front door with their wallets in hand, your marketing should be all about YOUR business.

Whether or not you fly a co-op's flag over your door should be secondary (though supportive of national advertising if at all possible) when considering the most effective way(s) to market

GIVING YOUR CUSTOMERS THE ROYAL TREATMENT

YOUR store.

As you digest all these facts and figures, read the next few chapters with an eye to "it's all around us" to pick up on some really brilliant, easy-to-implement and insanely effective strategies that you can tweak to fit your business.

I'll catch up with you in the last chapter and give you some concrete examples of promotional products your hardware store brethren have used to great advantage over the course of the 40 years UniSource has been serving the industry...

PHIL BRAKEFIELD

About Phil Brakefield

Phil Brakefield is a published author, speaker, consultant and trainer with more than forty years of experience in serving the independent hardware store trade through his company, UniSource.

Phil is known as the "Wizard of Widgets" and the "Guru of Garments"...titles earned because of his unmatched expertise in both the promotional products and apparel categories.

Thousands of independent hardware stores look to Phil's creativity for high quality, cost-effective, laser-targeted, response-boosting solutions to their marketing and branding challenges.

At all times, Phil is a bursting-at-the-seam proud Dad and Grandfather.

And in his spare time, he also serves on the board of the Chicagoland Dog Rescue, is a passable guitar player, a fidgety drummer, an awful banjo player (in learning mode), inconsistent golfer, music freak, photography wonk, insatiable

GIVING YOUR CUSTOMERS THE ROYAL TREATMENT

seeker of marketing education, and the proud owner of a wicked sense of humor.

The humor thing often comes in handy when trying to deal with corporate types...

especially if the nameplate on the office door says Marketing Department.

To reach Phil, you can contact him directly at:

www.Unisource-Promos-Club.com

Phil@Unisource-Promos-Club.com

Phone: (800) 859-2831

Fax: (847) 458-1932

Chapter 4

Why Your Marketing Should Be As Unique As Your Business

By Mary Forte

Are your customers knocking down your doors begging to do business with you? Are you always looking for new customers because your current customers do not shop as often as they used to?

In case you haven't noticed, retail has changed tremendously since the "Global Recession of 2008." If you are doing the same things you've always done, and expecting to get the same results you had before the recession…you must read on.

There is no room for the "doing enough to get by" attitude in business today. To succeed as a successful retailer in today's economic environment you must have total unwavering commitment and determination to change.

When you opened your business, you probably created it with a distinct vision and to run in a specific manner. You may still be using that same model, as if some law exists forbidding its change.

Our New Economy dictates a more assertive, proactive entrepreneur. You must be willing to adapt a creative approach and be open to constant change in order to keep your business fresh and relevant to the consumers walking in your doors. An agile business, run by an agile leader, can be very successful in today's economy.

GIVING YOUR CUSTOMERS THE ROYAL TREATMENT

Here are four realities of retail in the New Economy:

1. The customer's tolerance for the ordinary is Zero.
   Our customers today are looking for exciting, entertaining, and enjoyable, products, services and education.

2. The customer has the power; they know it, they demand it.

3. Money is being spent more cautiously.
   People have the opportunity, power, and awareness to find products matched to their needs, interests and desires. Products are often researched online before the consumer walks into your doors.

4. Purchasers determine if you are:
   - Worthy of their trust
   - Knowledgeable about the products you sell
   - Offering the level of service they are seeking

I Learned Them All the Hard Way!

I believed my customers would shop with me because they liked my store and the brands we had to offer.

The entire staff was always friendly and helpful. We knew our product lines well, and offered great customer service, but that was not enough.

The BIG SECRET is in MARKETING your business. I'm not talking about a weekly e-blast to your list; although necessary, it is not enough to sustain a successful retail business. Again, take it from the woman who learned that lesson the hard way.

MARY FORTE

In 2008, I was strapped for cash when my husband of 30 years decided he no longer wanted to be married, and left.

We were a "mom & pop" Sewing Center. I was the creative side of the business, selling machines, teaching classes, scheduling events and guest teachers. He was the business side, doing the books, marketing, and advertising. There was no business plan, marketing plan, or budget left behind to guide me after he was gone.

I kept hearing about the impact of email marketing and started to build a list of customer emails. Because I was left with a mountain of debt, it was the most cost effective way to stay in touch with my customers.

I was so excited the day my list reached 1,000 e-mail addresses! Then it doubled and tripled!! However, EVERY business in the world jumped on the email marketing bandwagon and people became inundated with offers streaming to their in-boxes. I had over 3,000 names on my list, but less than 800 people were actually opening them. Moreover, these were people who have shopped in my store and opted into the list.

I was stunned – These were avid sewing enthusiasts, and I was offering them great information, coupons and classes. Why wouldn't they pay attention to the emails I was sending?

Sometimes we get so self-absorbed in running our business day to day that we can't look beyond our own doors.

I was reading my own personal emails one evening when it hit me. I was deleting many emails without ever opening them even though I opted into the lists! We are all on information overload, and have a limited amount of time to spend sorting through our in-boxes.

GIVING YOUR CUSTOMERS THE ROYAL TREATMENT

They key to a better open rate is all about the Headline (subject line) of the email. You must grab the attention of your readers in that one line!

You should start keeping a list of Headlines that grab your attention and make you want to open the email and read more. You can then modify it to suit your business.

Once I realized my email marketing was not bringing customers in the door as expected, I knew I needed to do something different.

I attended a local marketing event in the Chicago area and met a man who was a wealth of information on marketing strategies for small business. I faithfully attended every event where he was teaching. Once I began implementing some of the things I learned and saw the results, I knew I was on the right track.

I was hungry for more.

Several years ago the opportunity arose to have him become my business coach. I jumped at the chance and have seen increased business growth ever since. Although he had no experience in the Retail Sewing Business, we have worked together to create many successful Marketing Campaigns to grow sales.

By doing more direct response marketing, my business has increased to over 1.5 Million dollars in sales. This has given me the ability to hire a full time manager and additional part time staff, which in turn, allows me to spend more time working *on* my business rather than *in* my business.

In the following pages I will share just a few of the Marketing pieces I have sent to my customers, which have brought substantial profits back into my business.

MARY FORTE

You Have Worked Very Hard to Build Your Customer Base.

They are the easiest customers to sell to because you already have a relationship with them.

In today's fast-paced world, you must keep the face of your business in front of people or they're going to forget about you.

One of the best ways to do this is through personalized direct marketing. When you personalize your Marketing Messages to your customers, it makes them feel special.

One of the Marketing Campaigns that I have implemented is our *Lost Customer Campaign.* It is very cost effective and the Return on Investment (R.O.I.) is amazing.

In our business, we consider a customer "lost" if they have not shopped with us in the last eight months. A three-step campaign begins at month #9. A personalized letter goes out to each customer.

The letter begins with an attention getting Headline, a personalized greeting, and includes the date of their last visit to the store. Also included in the letter are two $10 Gift Certificates, also personalized using the mail merge function in your word processing program.

The Gift Certificates expire two weeks from the date of the letter. (Remember, we are a brick & mortar store with mostly local customers. So the customer most likely will receive it the next day).

A second step is sent on the expiration date of the first letter. It also has an attention-getting headline and the same personalization as the first letter. The same two Gift Certificates

GIVING YOUR CUSTOMERS THE ROYAL TREATMENT

are in the letter with the same two-week expiration.

The third step is the same as step two, but has a "last chance" headline and Gift Certificates. It also asks for feedback if there is a reason they no longer shop with us.

We very seldom get all the way through to the last step. If the customer comes in to redeem the Gift Certificates after step #1 or #2, the mailing sequence stops.

Another very successful Marketing Campaign is our *Referral Campaign.*

Just think of how many times you make a purchase, or eat at a restaurant because a friend recommended, or "Referred" that business to you.

Referral customers are the easiest customers to sell, and are usually your best customers.

Every time we have a large ticket sale, we send out a thank you note. Yes, you guessed it! Every note is personalized and thanks the customer for their purchase. If it is a Sewing Machine or Software purchase, we remind them to sign up for their Free Lessons.

Included in each note is a FREE Admission to our monthly Sewing Club, and two Referral Cards. The cards are business card sized so they can easily fit into a wallet. The next time our customer talks about their new purchase to a friend, it's easy to pull out the referral card with all the store information on it.

When the new referral makes a purchase from the store, a thank you gift goes out to the loyal customer who recommended them to us.

MARY FORTE

Another successful Marketing Campaign is our *Trade-Up Campaign*.

Every quarter we go through our machine sales records and send letters to select customers offering a trade-up value for their old machine. Every letter has the make & model of their current machine, the original purchase date, and the amount we will give them towards a trade-up to a new, *model specific*, machine.

This Marketing Piece is also very cost effective and has a Huge R.O.I. (Return on Investment).

You can't market any business on a hope and a prayer!

Marketing a business is all about getting customers in the door and spending money. I no longer *hope* someone will walk into our store and *pray* they'll buy something. I make it happen with all the marketing systems I have put into place for my business.

I have put together a multi-faceted support program for entrepreneurs just like you. It is designed to help Sewing Centers, Quilt Shops, and Vacuum Dealers use Direct Marketing systems to position their business for maximum success.

If you are interested in learning how to keep the customers that you have, bring more customers through your doors, increase your sales, and raise your profit margins, then contact me today.

GIVING YOUR CUSTOMERS THE ROYAL TREATMENT

About Mary Forte

Mary Forte is the owner of the largest independently owned Sewing Center in the greater Chicago area. She has been able to grow her retail store into an extremely profitable business.

How did Mary obtain such a deep understanding of marketing campaigns? Necessity...

Like many small businesses, Mary and her husband ran their retail store together. In 2008 her husband of thirty years left; he not only left the marriage, he also left behind a mountain of business and personal debt.

She had two choices: sink or swim. She decided to paddle as fast as she could!

Mary had to learn everything possible about running her Sewing Center more profitably. She needed to get lots of customers in the door fast, and all of them spending money. Better profit margins would help pay off the debt quickly.

The economy was falling and the old methods of advertising were no longer working.

MARY FORTE

She hired a business coach who specialized in small business marketing, and started creating and implementing marketing campaigns. She discovered the key to bringing in more business was better marketing.

With the guidance of her coach, she quickly learned how successful marketing campaigns were the secret to better profits and "customers for life."

Mary has grown her business from the 3,600 square foot store she owned in 2008 to a 14,000 square foot specialty retail store. She has more than doubled her sales, and they continue to increase every year.

Her unique "out of the box thinking," coupled with her proven marketing systems are why you should listen to her. She knows what works and what doesn't, because she has "been there and done that!"

Mary is clearly the expert when it comes to understanding the independent retailer niche. Her methods will have your small business swamped with customers.

If you are ready to market with confidence, contact Mary at: **BizCoach@MaryForte.com and *Check out Mary's Bonus Offer on the next page:***

Bonus Offer

For a *Free* copy of my E- Book

***"TURN YOUR CUSTOMERS INTO CASH MACHINES!
How Raving Fans Increase Your Bank Account"***

send an email request to

BizCoach@MaryForte.com

Chapter 5

Leader Of The Pack

By Jon Bockman

*'Don't follow the pack because the
view from the back isn't that great.'*

Direct marketing has been around for longer than we can even conceive. I like to think that the first direct marketing campaign started with word of mouth.

Then it progressed to flyers in local shops. Next there were newspaper ads as well as yellow page ads. These were pretty much the basics, and they seemed to do well.

But as the world started changing, so did marketing ways. Many people don't even read the newspaper anymore. They get their news online.

The same with the telephone book. I can't remember the last time I even saw one in my house! Just go to www.yellowpages.com and you've got access to phone numbers and addresses to anything, anywhere.

With the new generation of customers, it's time to figure out a new generation of marketing.

My New Direct Marketing

I started doing direct response marketing about 4 yrs. ago. At that time we were in a little 3-bay gas station, barely doing about $400,000 a year in sales.

By starting to do more direct marketing I was able to hire my

GIVING YOUR CUSTOMERS THE ROYAL TREATMENT

first service writer. This allowed me to work more _on_ my business than _in_ my business. Because I was available to spend my time where it was needed we were then able to grow the business and move to a new location.

In 3 years I was able to take our business to over $1Million in sales. It all came down to getting quality clients, and getting the ones that I wanted, not just someone who had car keys and could fog a mirror.

When I moved our location to the border of the two towns of Sycamore and DeKalb, I was able to not only keep our existing customers, but we were able to pick up a lot of business from Sycamore.

I know that moving our location helped with our increase, but we couldn't have gotten the people there without letting them know we were there. By marketing our business we went from about 150 repair tickets a month to well over 330 repair tickets today.

I knew that in order to bring in more business I had to do something "out of the box". That's why I came up with 3 campaigns that have worked wonders for us:

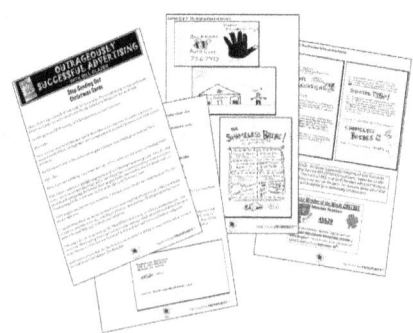

JON BOCKMAN

1) Thanksgiving Cards
2) "IRS" Check
3) Christmas In July

1. Thanksgiving Card

To give you an idea of what we sent out, here are some ideas (as drawn by my most talented son!):

When my son Owen was about 8 years old, I had him hand draw Thanksgiving cards to send out to customers and prospects.

We included a hand written letter with the card that thanked our clients for their continued support. We also let them know what was going on with our business.

And of course, we also included our famous "Shameless Bribes" coupon to bring our customers flooding in!

GIVING YOUR CUSTOMERS THE ROYAL TREATMENT

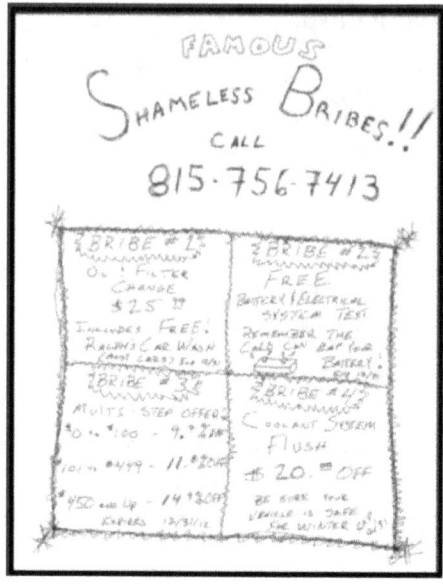

In the few years this one repeating marketing piece has brought in over $409,832 in revenue.

This has worked because people never expected to receive a Thanksgiving card.

Because most businesses send out Christmas cards, they tend to get lost with everyone else's cards. And they generally do not to include any offers for their clients.

Not only did we have the element of surprise, but it made us stand out from everyone else. It was such a remarkable campaign that we were actually featured in Dan Kennedy's No B.S. newsletter!

JON BOCKMAN

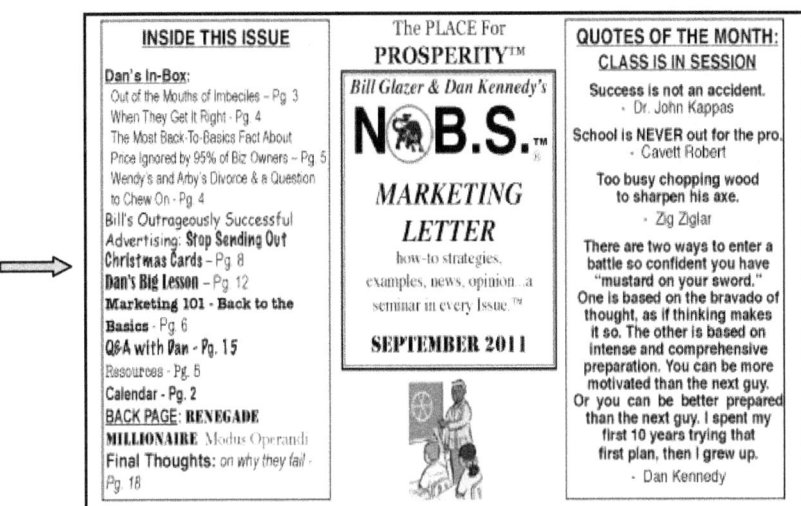

2. "IRS Check"

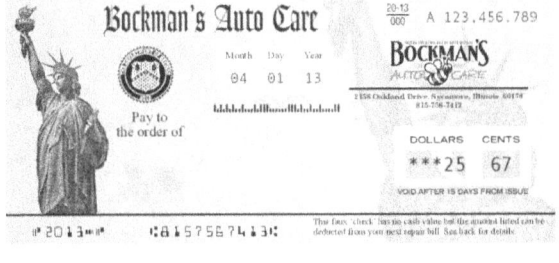

This is what I like to call "Sneak Up" mail. This is one piece of mail that gets opened!

GIVING YOUR CUSTOMERS THE ROYAL TREATMENT

Every April we send out an envelope which looks exactly like an IRS refund check.

Everyone is thinking they are getting money back from the boys at the IRS.

I put different values on each check, and people can use them to get discounts on our services.

The IRS promotions alone bring us about $35,000 in business every single year.

3. **Christmas in July**

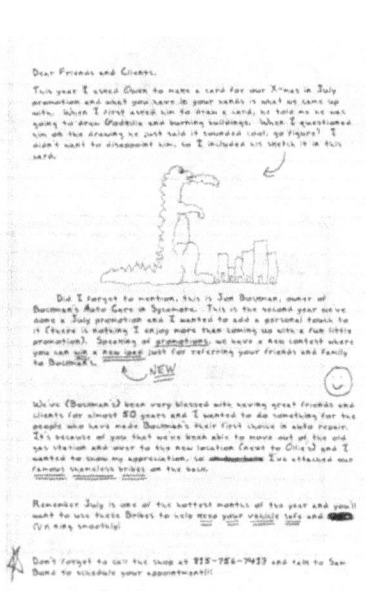

JON BOCKMAN

Have you ever gotten a Christmas card in July? Neither did any of our clients.

Until we sent one out, that is!

Once again I had my son, Owen help. He drew a picture of Santa on a beach, by the ocean.

And of course we included a hand-written letter and our "Shameless Bribe" coupons.

GIVING YOUR CUSTOMERS THE ROYAL TREATMENT

A couple of reasons I feel this works so well:
1. Holiday events are emotional triggers for people; they think of friends, family and younger days.
2. It gives a good reason "why" people should buy, because deals are expected around the holidays.

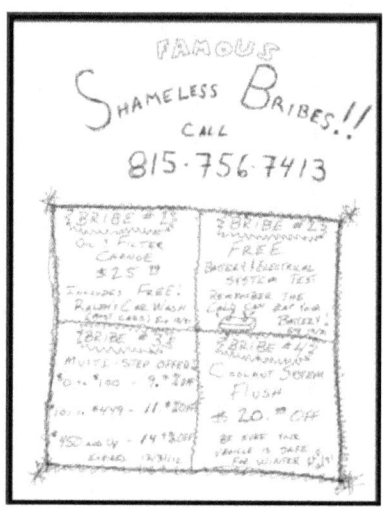

This ONE piece generated over $43,000 last year alone!!

As you can see, just these three pieces have had a huge impact on my business.

Getting the Word Out

One of my favorite quotes is from the movie The Hangover – *"I tend to think of myself as a one-man wolf pack"*.

That still touches my funny bone when I hear it, even though the message is not really funny at all.

There's no reason to do everything by yourself.

Hiring my service writer gave me the time to commit to my business. It may not be an option for everyone, but committing to marketing has to become MY new job.

Could I have still made the move without the extra help? Probably.

But how long would it have taken me? Would I still be at the old place telling myself "just another couple of months?"

I think I would.

Here's the bottom line…

You need to find ways to separate yourself from the pack. Think outside of the box.

Ask yourself every day, "What can I do that's different from my competition? What can I do to make myself stand out from the crowd?

For me, it came to the point where other owners kept asking me how I did it.
How did I double my business?
How did I triple my time off?

How did I get my life back, and have the peace of mind I never had before?

So, to answer all of them, I put together a program to help other auto repair shop owners get the same results I did.

GIVING YOUR CUSTOMERS THE ROYAL TREATMENT

And I have to say, I really love helping other auto repair shop owners achieve a new level of income and lifestyle.

So if you want to learn how to drive in more customers, keep the customers that you have, and raise your bottom line, then contact me today at **HighTorqueMarketing.com** so we can start you on your road to increased success.

JON BOCKMAN

About Jon Bockman

Jon Bockman is President and CEO of both High Torque Marketing and Bockman's Auto Care. He is an experienced entrepreneur with over 29 years in the automotive industry.

Jon took his small local repair shop and in less than four years increased its sales by 125%, to over $1,000,000. His new passion is to help other auto repair shop owners turn their struggling businesses around.

Jon's success with his marketing efforts is a direct result of his creativity and innovation. He was awarded "Marketer of the Year" for 2011 and 2012 by the Chicagoland's Sharpest Entrepreneurs. This bright group of nearly 200 business owners, marketers, and entrepreneurs elected Jon based on his greatly successful marketing for Bockman's Auto Care. In 2012, Bockman was a national runner up for GKIC's "Marketer of the Year."

Jon also hosts a local radio talk show, *"Garage Radio with Jon Bockman,"* where he answers questions about automotive repair.

GIVING YOUR CUSTOMERS THE ROYAL TREATMENT

Jon resides in northern Illinois with his wife and two sons. He holds a second degree in black belt and is involved with the local baseball program.

For information on how you can turn your auto repair shop into a predictable sales machine, or to learn about Jon's products and coaching, connect at **www.HighTorqueMarketing.com**.

Bonus Offer

For a

FREE 15 Minute Consultation,

PLUS

$500 OFF
Jon's Auto Repair Swipe File System,

contact Jon at

815-901-0276

Chapter 6

Live the Life of Your Dreams After You're 65:

Three Big Mistakes that Retiring Professionals Make that Keep them Wondering What They'll Do next and Whether They'll Be Bored in Retirement

By Russell Burck

I started thinking about retirement when I was 63. I didn't expect to retire at 65, but I got started with an online business several months before my 64th birthday. That didn't go anywhere. I retired in 2008 from my career, and in 2011, at age 73, I tried again to become an entrepreneur. I thought I had found a fast track, but I have painfully learned that it was a detour. Luckily, I have a coach and a supportive group of budding entrepreneurs who are helping me find my true path.

This chapter seeks to help you, as a senior citizen and retiring professional, to create income, learn new skills, and deepen your access to your inner powers. It examines three big mistakes that you can make as you are retiring. These mistakes can keep you puzzled about what step to take next: focusing too narrowly on finances, bracing yourself for boredom, and dwelling in denial when a mentor would lead you out. This chapter will say what each mistake is, why it's important to know about it, and how you can do something about it now. At the end, the chapter offers to help you if you're thinking about becoming an entrepreneur.

Mistake #1: Focusing on Finances

What is "focusing on finances?" Merriam-Webster.com defines focus as "a center of ... attention."

GIVING YOUR CUSTOMERS THE ROYAL TREATMENT

On eHow.com, Bonnie Conrad writes, "Perhaps the biggest retirement pitfall is the risk of running out of money... to enjoy a comfortable retirement."

My minister told me the congregation's elderly often said that. Before I retired from Rush, quite a few people said, "I wish I had enough to retire on." In all likelihood, you yourself have asked, "Do I have enough to retire on?"

Why can it help you to see that focusing on finances is a mistake? After all, finances have been integral to your adult life. In retirement, it will probably be harder to improve your finances, so of course you'd focus on them.

Here's why it's a mistake. Some of us had entrusted retirement funds to the bankers and brokers who put our economy into recession in 2008. If you focus on that, you can become a victim. Being a victim can narrow your field of vision to your biological, physiological, and safety needs. Considering yourself a victim, you can worry yourself awake at 2 a.m. In the power of victimhood, it's easy to forget everything that's going well, forget gratitude, forget how beautiful the world is, forget that there's more to life than food, water, shelter, clothing, your meds, and safety.

When I focus on finances and having the bare necessities I forget belonging and love, esteem, and self-actualization (Abraham Maslow, *A Theory of Motivation*) even though these require little money. I forget my beloved maternal grandmother who, having little, became a blessing to everyone she met.

The following chart shows the high costs of zooming in tightly on finances. My wife Dorothy and I paid this price:

Item	Cost
I imagined I could make a lot of fast promoting merchant accounts. That didn't pan out.	Financial Loss Loss of sleep Stress Embarrassment that I picked a bad area to work in.
Dottie kept telling me that I was kidding myself.	Inwardly fighting the truth. Damage to my relationship with Dottie, the love of my life. Self-delusion: I thought I had understood and done due diligence.
We lacked money to travel.	A favorite pleasure.
I wasted nearly 18 months looking for a suitable business.	My only irreplaceable resource—time.

Peter Orszag, Barack Obama's former director of the Office of Management and Budget, published an article in the June 11, 2013 issue of Bloomberg.com, "Retirement Will Kill You." Of the many comments that his article produced, this one improves the balance in my focus on finances:

What I find interesting is that we see columns every week about

GIVING YOUR CUSTOMERS THE ROYAL TREATMENT

'will we outlive our savings.'

Do you know what I never see?

'Will we die before we have a chance to enjoy our savings?' And I don't mind working, but if it is just so I can leave a bigger inheritance, what's the point?

That being said, now let's turn to the question: **How** can you address those middle-of-the-night worries about retirement? Right now?

> 1. Acknowledge that focusing on finances builds your happiness on a false assumption; namely, happiness comes after we have a sufficient accumulation. Actually, happiness comes first.
>
> 2. Face the pain that we have lost irreplaceable time trying to get what we need "to be happy."
>
> 3. See the dawn. Welcome the spring of new chances.
>
> 4. If you're so inclined, do the due diligences that will help you find an entrepreneurial opportunity that can succeed, and that fits you.

Mistake #2: Bracing for Boredom

The second pitfall, Ms. Conrad says, is boredom. **What** is bracing for boredom? Once again, Merriam-Webster.com defines *boredom* as "the state of being weary and restless through lack of interest." *Bracing* is steeling yourself. Bracing yourself for boredom in retirement would be steeling yourself to weariness, to restlessness, and to a world devoid of interesting things.

Why does it matter that we pay attention to the possibility that we are bracing ourselves for boredom in retirement? Looking at retirement that way can make us feel as if we're looking at the desert for the first time. There's nothing there. Endless waves of sand or barren soil, scrubby plants, creatures that can kill us, skeletons, and almost none of one of life's essentials—water.

When I see that, I think b-o-ring. I feel afraid. When I was 14, our family moved from desert country in northern New Mexico to urban New Jersey. I missed my home, but not the desert.

If I were to imagine my retirement as life in the desert, I'd catch the next caravan out. That picture of retirement could wake me up in the middle of the night, despairing about what I'm going to do in retirement.

Some people work full weeks and long hours. Often, from one working day to the next, they retire completely. Cold-turkey. An eHow blogger says that these workers switch from an organized workday to a near-total lack of structure. I hope that you can ease into retirement part-time.

To me, cold-turkey retirement is like the astronaut's being set adrift in *2001*. It's like Wile E. Coyote racing past the edge of the cliff, off into space, and into the mercy of gravity. There goes our support.

On retirement-cafe.com, Ernie Zelinski examined an app that purports to tell people their "number." Your number shows "the amount you will need to have saved to retire the way you want." Zelinski's own number wasn't going to let him retire the way he wanted.

But Zelinski isn't saying, "Oh my, oh my." He writes,

GIVING YOUR CUSTOMERS THE ROYAL TREATMENT

"This 'simple' retirement calculator is also apparently *wrong* in my case. My retirement life is retirement living at its best — having the *freedom* to do what I want when I want and still having some *enjoy*able retirement *work* to keep my *mind alive* and *creative*."

Boredom does occur in retirement, like duh, but it doesn't have to dominate it.

How can you avoid boredom? You probably have a list of activities, so you know the answer, as least, in part. Here's some additional truth—someone like Zelinski can guide us:

- Zelinski **names** what he wants in retirement—freedom, enjoyment, vitality.

- He **notices** that he already has what he wants. What would keep you from doing that right now?

- Zelinkski doesn't say he's **grateful**, but he sounds grateful. We can all be grateful right now.

I don't remember feeling bored just before I got into promoting merchant services after Dottie and I took our next-to-last vacation in 2011. But I do remember being excited and self-affirming because I would be in a business of my own. You can have that kind excitement, too. Just do your due-diligence and you'll find an entrepreneurial niche that works for you.

Mistake #3: Dwelling in Denial and Missing a Mentor

Zelinski says that the number calculator he used is wrong. It's not telling all the truth that we need. It is true that we need an accumulation of resources, but the truth is much bigger than that. If Zelinski settled for the truth about accumulation alone, he'd be "dwelling in denial."

What is "dwelling in denial?" Our old friend Merriam-Webster.com says that "dwell" means "to remain for a time." It also means "to keep the attention directed" toward. "Denial" means "refusal to admit the truth or reality."

Dwelling in denial means remaining in a place where our attention is directed toward not admitting "truth or reality."

What is "missing a mentor?" A mentor is a "trusted counselor or guide." To miss is to "discover . . . the absence of" (Merriam-Webster.com). Missing a mentor is discovering that we're not getting the benefits of having a counselor to guide us into entrepreneurship.

Why is "dwelling in denial" something to avoid?

What matters most in the world is this one thing: Loving the truth for its own sake.

We've all lived such ostrich or turtle lives that becoming clear about what's true is one of our most difficult tasks. For many of us the "truth" of our life is that we are condemned to being failures and to dwelling in the land of failure. Many of us never question that "truth." A similar "truth" is that we're stuck here with no one to help us get out. Likewise, we believe that wealth and spirit are on planes that never meet.

What is the truth about entrepreneurship? It's about more than material wealth. It's spiritual. One meaning of spirit is self-transcendence: Getting outside ourselves, looking at ourselves, telling ourselves the truth. Getting outside ourselves, we see

GIVING YOUR CUSTOMERS THE ROYAL TREATMENT

others' needs, we create ways to help them meet those needs, and we get paid for these services. Entrepreneurship advances others' well-being.

What truth is there to love about being an entrepreneur? In addition to doing the things just mentioned, you can learn many interesting things. If you've been a writer, you can become a better writer. If you've avoided marketing, you may find marketing fascinating. But most of all, you can learn that you have powers and vision that others value. You are far more original and creative than you can imagine.

Why is it important to become aware that missing a mentor is a mistake? I'll use myself as an example—only through my coach did I learn that "All successful entrepreneurs have coaches," including him.

He and the colleagues in my mastermind group are helping me become an entrepreneur. After years of feeling like a failure, I am learning that I am a "success-in-progress." I'm learning how to make some of my many ideas valuable to other people. I've always thought that I'd have to live on the outskirts of wealth, yearning for it, but I'm discovering that my gifts can create win-win situations for other people, and for myself.

How can you do something about dwelling in denial and missing a mentor? Short answer: "Move out." You can learn how you give yourself a present when you see that you've dwelt in the land of falsehood and pretense. Yes, you'll miss it. It was home for a long time.

And if you're like most people, you'll need friends to help you love. A good mentor will tell you, "This is going to take a while.

Let it take as long as it takes. The big thing—get moving." Do something. Do it with a guide.

Now in this later chapter of my life, I'm becoming re-acquainted with myself. I'm becoming reconnected to my energy and passion, which I had almost given up on.

I'm offering you a chance to experience something similar. You can learn what's true in your life. You can learn that discovering painful truths about yourself pays you better than avoiding it. You can learn that you have gifts and abilities that you have forgotten or completely overlooked. You can learn again how much fun there is in learning.

One of these days you'll look at yourself in the mirror and say, "Good for you. I know you hated to remember that event, I know you felt bad when you relived that regret and that wishing that you hadn't done something. Relax, breathe in, and breathe out. Listen to me. That took courage. That took strength. That took compassion and kindness toward yourself. You gave yourself hope that facing pain would open up into, well, into joy, joy that's here right now. Before long you'll be noticing a bit of peace."

It's encore time for us older people. Let's do it. Let's do it together. Now.

GIVING YOUR CUSTOMERS THE ROYAL TREATMENT

About Russell Burck

Russell Burck is a retired minister. He taught pastoral care in Germany and served as chaplain; Associate Professor of Religion, Health and Human Values at Rush University Medical Center, Chicago; and head of the Ethics Consultation Service.

He served on the faculty and board of Rush's Geriatric Interdisciplinary Team Training, in which resident physicians and graduate students of nursing, social work, and other disciplines studied team care of geriatric patients.

Russell has also contributed chapters to *Ethical Patient Care: A Casebook for Geriatric Health Care Teams.*

In retirement Russell writes, speaks, and coaches other retirees about living a full life in retirement, including the joys of becoming an entrepreneur.

Russell is enjoying his action packed "golden years" with his beautiful bride of nearly 53 years, Dottie. They also enjoy spending time with their 2 children, Peter and Lise, and their spouses, Susan and Allen. They'd love to have grandkids, but that doesn't seem to be in their future - yet. Until problems with their finances in Oct, 2011, they traveled one week each month for three years. He has written about some of these travels in his blog, *Scribbler's Travels*, which you can see at **www.ScribblersTravels.com.** Russ is still working on some of these stories, which include trips to Newfoundland; Labrador; the Yukon; Denali, the Arctic Circle, and Denali National Park in Alaska; Sedona, AZ; Australia and New Zealand.

Dottie loves gardening and feeding and watching birds. As a retired math teacher, she is super into sudokus. Russ loves photography, sudokus, and his most recent project—"living the truth."

So, if you would like to explore your own desire for hope and possibility in retirement, contact Russell today at **www.RussellBurck.com.**

Bonus Offer

($497 Value)

For a

Free 1 hr Consultation

enter your email address at

www.RussellBurck.com/bonus

GIVING YOUR CUSTOMERS THE ROYAL TREATMENT

"DO YOU REALLY INSIST ON DOING EVERYTHING YOURSELF, DOCTOR?"

Chapter 7

Pain Management for Business Success

By Bryan Regnier

Do you want to get more results and revenue for your business with less effort?

If you want to grow and expand your business or make it more efficient, then you need this chapter, because you can do all that and more with one simple solution I'll share with you in a moment.

The economy has been an excuse for most businesses for the last few years. Are you still using it as an excuse? Why? Do you believe the economy is going to come back so you can disregard looking for solutions?

I hate to break it to you, but you may be waiting a very long time. The economy will never be as strong as it once was, plus it is something that is totally out of our control. I'll admit, I used the same excuse for a while but I found solutions, and now I am no longer singing the same song and dance.

As entrepreneurs we go into business because we have a drive, a passion, and we love what we do. The key to success is focusing our attention on the things we do best and delegate the rest.

I am not here to tell you that you need to do this or that better in your business; I don't know your business, therefore, I have nothing to tell you regarding that. However, I am here to tell you that there are *better ways* to do the things within your business.

GIVING YOUR CUSTOMERS THE ROYAL TREATMENT

As business owners, we have tasks and duties that consume our daily lives. Things that we don't like doing that drain our energy, like working long hours, working harder and getting paid less, but yet we still do it.

It is hard for a business owner to relinquish the control of the tasks and duties in their business because they think no one can do as good of a job as they can. I am here to tell you that if you think that, you will never

...grow,

...expand, or

...increase revenue.

More than likely, these tasks consist of things that you could pay someone $9.00 to $15.00 an hour to accomplish.

But the question I have for you is...how much is your time worth?

Money can be replaced, but your time can't. Those menial tasks don't grow the business, increase profits, or decrease expenses. Running your business should not be a full-time job. Entrepreneurs are not looking for a job; they are doing what they love and living in financial freedom.

There are many people out in the world today who want a job who are willing to work for $9.00 an hour, or even less, depending on what you are looking for and where you are looking.

Of course, you can hire, train, and invest in an employee to work for $9.00-$15.00 an hour, plus payroll taxes, insurance, and benefits. You can also hire an independent contractor to do the same things without having to pay insurance, taxes, and benefits. But both of these examples will eventually give you problems that will hinder your business.

What happens if something life threatening occurs to one of them or they move on to the next best thing and you have nothing to fall back on? You have to go through the same hiring, training, and investing program you did before, make up for lost time, plus worry about the same thing happening again. This can add up to:

- lost profits
- reduction in lead generation
- lack of sales conversions
- lack of fulfillment
- delays in collecting your receivables

The same is true if you have a large staff in your office. Things get overlooked; it is part of any business, especially if you continue to dump more tasks and duties upon them. This happens quite often inside of medical practices.

Most staff members in a business are responsible for more than one job description, especially these days. It takes a very organized staff with systems in place to ensure timely accomplishment and fulfillment.

What effect would it have on your business if there was a more reliable and organized solution to these issues? In some cases, the previous examples may work for your business, but for others who run more elaborate operations or need more sophisticated specialization, they need to find a more comprehensive, innovative, and established solution.

GIVING YOUR CUSTOMERS THE ROYAL TREATMENT

In our complicated world, there is nothing that you cannot find that can't be done more efficiently with increased flexibility, increased productivity and reduced costs better than *Outsourcing*.

Outsourcing can provide great benefits to a business's operations. With done-for-you services, the costs of doing business can decrease dramatically. Our economy is never at rest and with it comes always changing regulations, laws, and guidelines that must always be followed, understood, and complied with.

There are, however, some disadvantages to outsourcing (some more common than others, but also irrelevant if you have a great outsourcing company) which include:

- compromising confidential data
- lack of communication
- timeliness or delays
- quality of work not up to your standards
- language barriers (if you outsource overseas)

It is your responsibility to do your homework with whatever company you choose to outsource to. You need to trust whoever it is that you hire. Outsourcing overseas may not be the best alternative for you if you need a human resources service to interview potential employees or if you need a billing company who provides access to financials quickly, and want to speak to someone who speaks your language.

Hiring a company overseas to oversee your financials may not be the best alternative. But other tasks such as online marketing, where you pay someone to work for $3.00 an hour on oDesk.com, where you can monitor your outsourcers work via a work diary, may be a more cost effective solution.

With that being said, there are many advantages to outsourcing, such as:

- no more payroll taxes
- no more benefits
- no more insurance (workers compensation, errors and omissions, etc.)
- no more taxes
- no more training costs (new or ongoing)
- no more hardware/software costs
- no more IT support

Investing in an outsourcing firm, whether it be for marketing, billing, human resources, customer service or other related administrative duties can greatly reduce your expenses, increase your cash-flow, and provide a more efficient means of operating your business. It also gives you an extension of your team that you can leverage at your convenience.

Outsourcing gives you access to valuable resources when you need them. Most of the time you will receive a better quality service that gives you a higher level of productivity and results.

Outsourcing firms specialize in what they do, and in most cases that is all that they do. It is their duty to stay on the cutting edge and current with any laws, regulations, guidelines, etc...

This is a huge drawback from doing it in-house; you have to absorb the cost of training staff and constantly need to remain up-to-date and compliant with regulations, current laws and guidelines, depending on your situation.

GIVING YOUR CUSTOMERS THE ROYAL TREATMENT

Investing in an outsourcing firm can save you time, money, and prevent headaches such as audits and fines. They are going to allow you and your staff to focus your resources on providing a better patient experience and selling your products or services at the highest levels *(allows you to concentrate on your core business rather than supporting tasks)*.

Lastly, **depending** on what you are outsourcing, you will pay by the hour, project, or based on results, so if you don't get results, you don't pay, which will help you avoid cash-flow issues (this only applies to certain situations).

In the case of outsourcing, you want to work with a firm that is going to go above and beyond what you ask for, who provides extraordinary value. Make sure that you understand what is included in your partnership.

The key to utilizing outsourcing services is that you must be the judge on whether your business is going to benefit from taking this step. You must weigh the pros and cons and decide if this is going to be beneficial for your business.

Measure your strengths and weaknesses and compare them to industry benchmarks. If there is a significant reason for changing, put a list of action items together for change, such as:

- Identify the things that drain your energy
    - Scheduling
    - Billing
    - Payroll
    - Taxes
    - Marketing
    - Customer Service
    - Human Resources
    - IT Service

- Identify the things you need to be doing but you are not (you have too much to do and not enough time to do it)
    - Follow-Up
    - Generating Leads For Your Business
    - Converting Your Leads Into Clients
    - A/R Management and Collections
    - Support for your clients
    - Software Upgrades and Updates
    - Training your Staff
    - Hiring new staff
    - Etc...

How to Outsource in Six Steps

1. Identify what you want to outsource
2. Research potential outsourcing firms or companies for the tasks you are looking to outsource
3. Call the potential outsourcing firms you researched
4. Interview companies who best fit your needs and wants
5. Hire the company that best fits your business model
6. Work with your outsourcing firm to systematize your tasks

Outsourcing should be a system within your business.

It should run just as smooth, if not smoother than if you were doing it in-house. Every business, in a sense, is a system made up of a collection of processes that produce an intended end result.

GIVING YOUR CUSTOMERS THE ROYAL TREATMENT

The money you save by outsourcing will allow you to invest the money back into the business for growth and expansion.

In the following example you will find a case study of how a Medical Practice saved $34,520.00 per year when they outsourced their billing to us: (Note: We eliminated a number of expenses from their practice.)

Average Annual Costs for Physician Billing	In-House Costs	Outsourcing Costs
500 claims per mo. X 12 @ $100 x 7.83%	----	$46,980
1.5 Full-Time Billing Employees @ $15 hr.	$46,800	$0
Payroll Taxes	$3,300	$0
Worker's Comp Insurance	$600	$0
Errors and Omissions Insurance	$300	$0
Compliance Training Costs	$3,600	$0
Leave Coverage (3 wks. Temp @ $20 hr.)	$2,400	$0
Employee Benefits Package	$5,100	$0
HER/EMR Software, Training IT Support,	$19,400	$0
46% less expensive to outsource	$81,500	$46,980
Increased Revenue (MORE PROFIT!)	$34,520 per year	
All Numbers For In-House Expenses Were Rounded To The Nearest One Hundred		

The important thing to note is that this can be done for all administrative duties in your business, whether it be for billing, marketing, human resources, customer service, or other related duties.

Outsourcing things you don't specialize in is one of the most commonly overlooked mistakes small businesses make. They think they need to do everything in-house, which can contribute to why their businesses fail. Why increase your overhead and add expenses that you don't need?

The most successful entrepreneurs do the things they love doing and they delegate the rest. They understand that they must focus on the things that got them to where they are today and that is why they are successful. In the beginning you may have to wear many hats, but as you grow you must give up those duties in order to focus on the things that drive and lead your business to success.

GIVING YOUR CUSTOMERS THE ROYAL TREATMENT

About Bryan Regnier

Bryan Regnier is the founder and President of Pulse MBP (Medical Billing Professionals) Inc., a successful Revenue Cycle Management and Consulting firm responsible for transforming ordinary Private Medical Practices into extremely profitable organizations using unique strategies and techniques that dramatically increase Physicians' bottom lines. He is increasingly called upon by Private Medical Providers seeking guidance on the revenue cycle management of their practice.

Bryan's expertise is helping specialty medical practices trim the waste from their administrative tasks and duties and is known as the *"Reimbursement & Expense Doctor."* He is helping Private Practice Physicians overcome Healthcare reform, obtaining and improving reimbursement rates, eliminating administrative burdens of patient approvals, and implementing and integrating electronic health records (EMR/EHR), all of which helps increase the number of patients seen in a day.

He saw the hardship and demands that were being asked of private practice specialty physicians and he decided to confront these issues head on. He has built a process of successful systems that are guaranteed to save physicians time and money.

BRYAN REGNIER

You can contact Bryan at **262.298.4220,** or visit him at **Bryan.Regnier@PulseMBP.com**

FREE BONUSES!
Grab Your *Free Copy*

"*The 7 Hidden Secrets that are <u>GUARANTEED</u> to Increase Net Revenue in your Medical Practice*"
($47 Value)

Go to: www.PulseMBP.com

Discover profits that lie hidden in your practice, *<u>GUARANTEED!</u>*

<u>Mention this book</u> and receive a:

FREE Medical Practice Administrative Audit ($297 Value)

Email Audit@PulseMBP.com with

"Pain Management for Business Success" in the subject line.

GIVING YOUR CUSTOMERS THE ROYAL TREATMENT

"WE DON'T KNOW CRAIG LEACH, SO THAT'S OUR ATTEMPT AT A NEW MARKETING STRATEGY"

Chapter 8

Aacceling At Your Business

By Craig Leach

I guess I've always liked to get my hands dirty. Or maybe I just like to see how things work, and when they don't work, fix them.

Back in the 1980's I took automotive and business classes in college. Even back then I knew that it wasn't enough to just know how to work on cars. I knew that you also had to learn the business side to be successful.

While in school I worked for a year at a company as an apprentice engine rebuilder and then at a Quick Lube. After three years at the Quick Lube I became an assistant manager.

With taking care of the daily operations and getting hands-on experience, this only solidified my desire to own my own business! With no further opportunity for advancement, I had to move on.

My uncle took me away from there! The company he worked for had an opening for an apprentice mechanic working on lift trucks. So I made the move.

After numerous years of working on lift trucks, even though I enjoyed the work, I wasn't getting paid what I was worth. I knew it was time to pursue my dreams and do my own thing.

Having been a "grunt" for so long, I knew I needed to sharpen my skills. In the ever-changing world of automotive technology, the best thing that I could ever do was to go back to school. So in the fall of 2000 and spring 2001, I went back and took several auto repair courses, a computer class, and a SBA (small business

GIVING YOUR CUSTOMERS THE ROYAL TREATMENT

administration) class.

I knew that I was no longer cut out to work for anyone else, so now was the time to take the plunge and open my own shop.

In June 2001, I signed my first lease and established my company, Aaccel Emissions and Lube. What a rush! The building had 3 bays, and it was the old emissions test facility. (Being the only emissions testing facility in Will County, they moved to a larger location right across the street.)

I had planned on having my grand opening on Sept. 1, 2001, but I didn't have all my lifts put in yet, so I postponed until Oct. 1. Then 9/11 hit, and my grand opening didn't do too well. But I hung in there, and by the end of 2006 I was able to purchase the building and the property. Then came the market crash and housing bubble burst of 2008, and for the next few years I found myself, like many others, struggling.

While struggling through 2009, I knew things had to change. I had to start working *ON* my business instead of *IN* my business.

So I hired a Service Advisor! Hiring the Service Advisor gave me more time to focus on my marketing skills.

It was a struggle for a while, but once I found my focus, my business started to turn around. Our marketing techniques have brought the customers in, and my staff was giving excellent customer service, while building customer rapport. I am very pleased to announce that we are currently Will County's #1 Emissions Repair Facility!

3 Ways to Build and Grow ANY Business

1. The most common one that most of us focus on is to **increase the number of customers we have.** The more

new customer we have, the more sales we have.

2. **Frequency** - turning a onetime customer into a repeat client.

    If you have 100 customers buying from you once a year and you can get them all to come back in **one** more time per year, you have just **doubled** your business. **Two** more times per year and you just **tripled** your business.

3. **Increase transaction size** - Upsell, Upsell, Upsell!

    A big part of this - is doing the math. To start, you have to know what your average sale or transaction is. If you have 100 clients spending $10, you will have $1,000 of sales. If you get each of them to spend 10 dollars more per transaction, you have doubled your sales to $2,000. McDonalds is a great example of doing this with packaging the sandwiches into the meals and also asking if you'd like to supersize it.

If you consistently focus on all three things your business will grow!

Who is typically the highest cost, hardest to sell and least profitable customer?

The New Customer!

What does it cost you to get a new customer? If you spend $600 on some type of marketing piece, whatever it is, and you gain 10 new customers from it that would be $60 of cost for each new customer. Depending on what you sell, this may be a lot or it may be a little. It depends on what your average sale is. For my auto repair shop, it would be more cost effective for me to give away a $30 oil change to gain a new customer. This was very

GIVING YOUR CUSTOMERS THE ROYAL TREATMENT

difficult for me to swallow in the past, but do the math!

What I have learned is that the new customer is the most expensive to gain and can be the hardest to keep. First time customers are always cautious when doing business with you. They may think you may be out to rip them off. You have to make sure that you are not hard selling them. Their first visit is an introduction and you have to WOW them. It is very important to always give them a great experience. Building a business is about building relationships. Once they know you - like you - and trust you, to get them to purchase from you again may be just a little more than the cost of a stamp.

Who is your best customer?

The Repeat Customer

The Repeat Customer should always be referred to as a Client!

The marketing cost of a repeat client is far less than a new customer, so there is a great profit margin. With repeat clients you have built a relationship with them so they come in more frequently, tend to spend more and will talk about you to others.

This is the "who" a lot of new businesses fail to focus on; me being one of them. When I first started out we had no customer management software. Big mistake! If you're starting a business or are *in* business and you don't have a customer management system, **you have got to get one**. T*his is a must! Your Gold is in your data base.*

When starting out I focused on getting new customers. I figured that with taking care of their needs, customers would just automatically come back. Not always the case. With having a good customer management system you can track your client history. You need to know when a client is due to come in. If they don't come in, you can take multiple steps to get them back in. This leads to my next question.

Who is your second best customer?

The Referral Customer

What others say about you is 1,000 times more powerful than what you say about you. When a customer comes to you who was referred by a client, they already know what you're about. They are easier to work with, tend to be less resistant to purchase from you and they spend more than your normal first time customer. Referral clients also tend to refer you more because someone told them about you.

Who's next?

The Lost Customer

If you haven't seen someone in a while, they are considered to be a lost customer. Why have they become lost? There are several reasons that could have contributed to this, but the most common reason is that they just forgot about you. If you don't keep yourself in front of them on a regular basis, people will forget about you. Tony Robbins refers to this as "TOMA": Top of Mind Awareness. The lost customer can be brought back, but chances are slim. If you use a multi-step lost customer campaign, you may be able to get some of them back in. Keep reading for a tip to help prevent a customer from forgetting about you.

Growing Your Business

To successfully grow your business you have to be able to track your clients. You have to know the 80/20 rule - 80% of your

GIVING YOUR CUSTOMERS THE ROYAL TREATMENT

money comes from 20% of your clients. You have to know who your top clients are and do everything you can to make sure you don't lose them.

Tracking your customers is very important - tracking your marketing is just as important!

If you think of marketing as an expense, you need to reconsider. If you go to a bank and for every dollar you give them they give you 5 dollars back, wouldn't you do that all day long? If you're spending money on marketing and not making a positive return on investment (ROI), then yeah, it is an expense. But it shouldn't be! If you are tracking your marketing and you know you are **not** getting a good ROI, then you have to move those marketing dollars to something else that will work for you.

The best way to do this is to test, test, and test. It's best to send out a sample mailing before you spend thousands of dollars on a marketing campaign. With sending out a sample mailing you can try multiple versions of a marketing piece and see which one gets the best response. By tracking the results you can be sure that your marketing dollars are being spent wisely, guaranteeing a positive ROI and your success.

Over the years we have improved our marketing and in doing so have increased our customer data base. A key to success is making as many customers as possible into *repeat* clients. With emissions testing being only every other year, when we get these customers in, I have made it a priority to try and get them to return for all their maintenance and repairs on all their vehicles -- To become their "Guy."

Now let's talk about some marketing strategies and some things that pay off for us.

CRAIG LEACH

My Marketing Tips and Tricks

With tracking the customer source (how they found you) and tracking the marketing revenues by source, the following are some of my top performers:

1. **Location, Location, Location**
   I'm probably the luckiest auto repair shop in the county. Not only am I right next to the Louis Joliet Mall, but I am also across the street from the only emissions test center in Will County. With the great location we get new customers with emissions failures and other walk-in repairs on a daily basis. Now, not everyone will be able to get as great a location as I have, but just keep in mind your surroundings when you are starting or purchasing your business. Keep in mind that you can always move your business, but you can't move your location.

2. **Maintenance Package Club**
   Clients can join our maintenance package club for only $100 a year. This entitles them to four oil changes per year, plus $25 towards any "buyer's choice" repair. Free items include a pair of wiper blades, brake inspection and tire rotation, battery/charging and starting system test, and an A/C performance test. The card also comes with $160 of discounts that are good towards maintenance services. This card is valued at $460, and for $100 they are locked in for one year. So with seeing club members 4 times per year we can do a better job of maintaining their vehicles, and it also gives us the opportunity to sell more maintenance and repairs. The repeat client is your best customer!

GIVING YOUR CUSTOMERS THE ROYAL TREATMENT

Don't let them get lost! This leads to the tip I had mentioned above.

3. **Monthly News Letter**

   A monthly newsletter is a friendly, low cost way to stay in front of your customers. You have to make it fun. It shouldn't just be about the nuts and bolts of what you do. It should have some type of game, like a cross word puzzle. It should have interesting articles that everyone can enjoy. You can include your Client of the Month, a welcome to new customers section, a section thanking the list of clients that referred someone to you, and an article with something about you or what's going on in your life, to give it a personal touch. Of course it has to include a couple of different offers with a deadline. We have to be constantly in front of our clients. That way when they need something or are in conversation with others and the need for your business comes up you are at the top of their mind.

4. **ClearMechanic**

   ClearMechanic is an awesome mobile app that allows dealers and repair shops to "visually explain" repairs with real-time photos, videos and expert diagrams. Vehicle photos and videos are instantly posted online for review by customers, or they can be emailed or texted. This gives our customers proof of work that needs to be done. Since implementing this app we have seen an increase in our service repairs, it has lessened the time for clients to approve repairs and it has improved work flow. A picture is worth a 1,000 words.

5. **Shop Management Software**

   As I said earlier, you have to have a good customer management system. We use our software to send several different marketing pieces. We send out a "Thank You" letter every Monday to our new customers, welcoming them to the Aaccel family, thanking them for their patronage. The "Thank You" letter gives them a discount offer to get them to come back in for any declined recommendations, or can be used on another vehicle, with a 30 day expiration.

   Through our software we also generate a Recommended Services letter. This is scheduled to be generated 15 days after they have been in, except if they have a safety issue, then it is done on the following Monday. Like the "Thank You" letter, this letter also goes out every Monday. It has a declining offer, so the quicker they respond the more they save. This also expires in 30 days.

6. **Schedule The Next Appointment**

   Dentists do it, so why can't you? Oil changes need to be done every 3 months, or 3,000 miles. When the customer picks up their vehicle, our software schedules their next appointment and we give them a next appointment reminder card. When it gets close to their appointment, we send them a reminder postcard. Then we give them a phone call 3 days later and another reminder phone call the day before the appointment. People are busy; with giving them a phone call, most people appreciate the customer service.

7. **Referral Program**

   Every customer, whether new or existing, gets 2

referral cards with their name hand written on it, when finalizing their repair order. Also, within a few days everyone gets a hand written "Thank You" Card. Inside that envelope are 2 more referral cards with their name hand written on them.

All they have to do is hand them out to friends, family, neighbors or co-workers and that person will get a FREE oil change. When the referred person comes in with the card, then the original client gets rewarded with a FREE oil change and the card gets placed into a fish bowl and becomes an entry into our quarterly referral contest.

We have tied our quarterly referral contest into something new - our monthly celebration party. When people have to spend money on auto repairs it's never fun, so we want them to have fun at AACCEL!

8. **Calendar Events**

Each month we do something different for our customers and the community. We try and base it on what special occasion is happening that month. Let me explain what I mean:

- January and February - We send out rebate checks based on their previous year's purchases. We send a check that's good towards any service or repair. We also celebrate Valentine's Day by handing out Roses, and do a Valentine marketing campaign.

- March and April – We send out an "IRS Check" to our customers with a specific amount that they can spend in our shop. In March our theme is

Irish, so we celebrate St. Patty's Day. We have a party and have our 1st quarter referral contest drawing where we give away some great prizes. In April our theme is Easter. We have an Easter basket with plastic eggs and everyone gets to pick an egg when we finalize their repair order. The eggs have a promotion in them for their next service.

- May – Craig's Birthday Party (May 7th) and Mother's Day Party. We also send out Mothers Day **Wow Cards** - These are like plastic credit cards with a gift offer on it. They cost less than $1 each, are really easy to do and work great. Check them out @ **www.wowcards.com,** and tell them Craig sent ya.

- June - We have our Anniversary/Father's Day party. We have a cook-out with burgers and dogs and have our 2nd quarter referral contest. We give away a Barbecue Grill for Father's Day and other great prizes like a tablet, a family 4-pack of water park tickets, a family 4-pack for the local skating rink, tickets for a high-speed boat tour on Lake Michigan, local restaurant gift certificates, and more. We also have a Father's Day special for the month of June.

- July - We have our Christmas in July Party. We barbecue and give away a gift to all that attend.

- August - We have our Back-to-School Party. We barbecue and give away school back packs to the kids.

GIVING YOUR CUSTOMERS THE ROYAL TREATMENT

- September - We have a Labor Day special for the month. We give 10% off labor for the month. At the end of the month we do our Grand Opening Anniversary and our 3rd quarter referral contest drawing. We give away a flat screen TV, a tablet, and other great prizes.

- October – We have our Spooky Halloween Costume Party. We award prizes to the top 3 costumes, and we give away candy to all the kids.

- November – We thank our clients with a Thanksgiving Card Special, and we have our Thanksgiving Celebration Party. We also do a food drive - we ask that customers bring in a non perishable food item. We give them a discount off their purchase and then we donate the food to the local food bank for the holidays.

- December - We have our Christmas/New Year's Party. During the party we have our fourth quarter referral contest drawing. We give away a flat screen TV, a DVD player, a tablet, and other great prizes. For December we give our best clients a Christmas gift of a Wow Card - $50 off of any repair over 50 dollars.

There are many, many ways of marketing for new customers - TV, Cable TV, Radio, Newspaper, Billboards, Road Signs, Phone Books, Valpak, Clipper Magazine, Flyers, Door Hangers, Various Internet sites like Web Sites, Google, Yahoo, Bing, Yelp, Merchant Circle, Angie's List, Craig's List, and Social media sites like Facebook, Twitter, LinkedIn and many, many more.

The question is - which ones will work for you? How do you

know what message to present, in what media, to what market? What is your budget? Do you have a budget? How do you get started?

Who can help you figure this all out?

Remember at the beginning when I said that I liked to fix things? Well, since we've increased our business in the last few years, I've had other shop owners come to me and ask how I did it. Not being a selfish person, I decided to help other owners that have struggled the same way I have.

My Final Words

As you can see I have talked about some of the things we do to keep and serve our current clients. There are more! I've talked about getting new customers by referral from current clients. The key to getting more referrals is you have to have a system in place, have a quality product/service, and YOU HAVE TO ASK! When someone thanks you for your service, let them know "The best 'thank you' you can give me is to tell another great client just like you about us!"

Keep in mind that it's not just one thing that you do, it's *multiple* things that help you increase your customer numbers and your bottom line. Keep testing your marketing strategies and track the results. If something doesn't work, either tweak it until it does, or just get rid of it. And stay on top of what does work.

I know that this year will be the best year I've ever had because I've made a decision to change things in my business. I know there are a lot of distractions every day, but it is ever so important to FOCUS on the things that will best improve your bottom line. Another important fact to remember is that the success of your business is not just how much sales you have,

GIVING YOUR CUSTOMERS THE ROYAL TREATMENT

but how much profit you keep and how much freedom you gain.

Never stop thinking of new ways to bring your customers in.

And if you get stuck, I have a bonus for you……

CRAIG LEACH

About Craig Leach

Craig Leach is the Owner/Operator of AACCEL Emissions & Auto Repair Specialists, Inc. This is a family owned and operated full-service repair and maintenance facility that has been performing high quality, guaranteed automotive repairs in the Joliet, Illinois area since 2001. Craig's shop repairs and services domestic and imported vehicles, and he prides himself on being "Will County's #1 Emissions Repair Facility!"

Craig earned his Automotive and Business degrees from Moraine Valley College in his home town of Palos Hills, Illinois. Over the past several years he has learned from various knowledgeable coaches, starting with Bob Cooper (Elite), Mike Lee (Management Success), Ron Ipach (CinRon), Gerry Frank and Keith McCrone (Automotive Profit Pro), Steve Sipress and his beautiful wife Michelle (ChicagoLands Sharpest Entrepreneurs) and has read and studied many books from authors like Napoleon Hill, Dale Carnegie, Dan Kennedy, Bill Glazer, Michael E. Gerber, Jon Gordon, John Maxwell, Spencer Johnson, Robert Ringer, Bob Burg and more.

While going to school, Craig worked part time as an apprentice

GIVING YOUR CUSTOMERS THE ROYAL TREATMENT

engine rebuilder, and then 3 years at a local Quick Lube. After graduating he was then promoted to assistant manager for the next 3 years. In 1994 he next went to work with his uncle as an apprentice working on lift trucks. Six years later he left the lift truck industry and returned to the automotive field to live his dream of owning his own repair shop.

Craig loves spending time with his family, and especially his adorable 6 year old daughter Leah.

To learn more about Craig and his business, check out his site at **www.Aaccel.com.**

Bonus Offer

For a *FREE*
($149 Value)

1/2 Hour Strategy Session

Just contact me at
Craig@Aaccel.com,

or fax me your info to

815-676-3026.

Chapter 9

How To Safeguard Your Clients Against The Unethical Competitor Out To Steal Their Money

A sure-fire formula for success... what the most successful contractors do

By John Senska

Back in 2005-2006, the housing market began a downward spiral into a complete crash, taking along with it many unprepared contractors. And like all avalanches, soon many parts of the economy followed suit. Banks failed, companies went out of business and people lost their jobs. With daily bad news reports and unemployment rising, a lot of people were worried about their own future. When people are scared they stop spending, which only drives the problems along.

Back then I was as much a part of the problem as anyone. As a builder/general contractor, I bought reasonably priced starter homes to knock down and build what was termed "mini-mansions". Sales were really good, and anyone with enough money to finance a new building became a contractor. Doctors, lawyers, traders, even tavern owners were calling themselves builders. Homes, condos or townhomes were selling faster than could be built. Heck, acres of land were developed and built on and often sold out before a third of the homes were even finished. We became our own best clients and sold only finished products.

While the market kept steadily declining, home inventory rose and home buyers disappeared. Not believing our great country would suffer long, many sat on the sidelines to wait it out. This plan only proved to put people further behind or completely out of business, since the bottom seemed elusive. It was very clear

GIVING YOUR CUSTOMERS THE ROYAL TREATMENT

that what this economy had was gone for good. The only way to survive was to change with it. I love challenges, but the idea of starting over at 47 years old didn't even come close to existing. However, having gone thru this way back during the Carter/Regan years, I was hopeful the pattern of recovery would be similar. Then at least I would have a place to start.

People will always need a place to live. Just like the great depression, people finally realized they couldn't wait any more. Things finally break or completely fall apart. Some may simply outgrow their space, but moving isn't an option. Everyone has a point at which they say enough is enough. It may take a while for people to reach this point, but it's always there. And sales people know this. A few will try to force you to this point by creating doubt or worry about the things you have lasting. Others keep making offers to coax you into making a decision, giving impressions of fantastic deals. All that really happens with these tactics is to create more mistrust in the market place. People have enough to worry about without having sales people use tricks and mind games. Now once trusted general contractors are looked upon as used car salesmen.

Before the gold rush of the housing boom, general contractors were trusted advisers in the community. It wouldn't be hard to find the right person to help you with your home's needs. If you asked a few neighbors or a family member who lives in the community, the same name most likely came up. Everyone knew that if you need "this" done, then you called so and so. These men knew they had to earn the trust of their communities or suffer.

Today, the digital age has changed the way things get done. Talking to friends and family may mean chatting online with people states away. Grocery shopping or ordering food for dinner is now only a couple of clicks away. Taking work home has also changed as more and more are working from home. Continuing your education can be done in the comfort of your own home.

Even after-hour events have changed from stopping with the guys or girls for a couple of drinks to meetings or classes, charity events or the gym. To add to already overloaded days, after you have children you begin to wish for all the time you thought you didn't have before.

So how do you not just get lost in people's daily lives? *Be a part of their lives.*

One way is to constantly throw advertisements at them. Newspapers, TV, radio, coupon books, go door to door, calling, maybe even a billboard. You could hire a larger sales force. Build fancier showrooms. Any one of these could work when people are ready for you. Strangely, they also may work for your competitors to take your clients away from you. We all like to believe our clients are loyal, but when it may be years between purchases, a lot can happen. For businesses like mine, do they even remember who it was the last time they had work done? Even if they remember, do they know how to get in contact with you? Worse yet, with the news puppets spewing bad news every day and companies going out of business, are you still around?

When the collapse started in the housing market, I realized I needed to adapt or disappear. I had to get my message out that I'm still here. Advertiser after advertiser all gave basically the same advice: branding. It's the same as standing on a bucket and yelling. Maybe someone will be interested. In a down market, there is a lot of yelling going on. Using dumb luck to attract new clients wasn't for me, but I also refused to give up.

GIVING YOUR CUSTOMERS THE ROYAL TREATMENT

As fortune would have it, I was given a free ticket to a seminar where Brian Tracy was speaking. At this seminar I was lucky enough to meet successful business leaders who in turn gave me advice on how to solve my problem. A Newsletter! Yeah, right, I thought. However, they were successful even in this economy and that's what I wanted. So with their help, I went to start a newsletter.

I started small, and it created a landslide. As advised, I started with past clients, people who already knew and trusted me. I stayed simple and just informed them about what was going on. As explained to me, it is not our clients' responsibility to remember us; *it's ours to remember them*. If you had a good relationship with your clients, you are more a welcome guest visiting than just some junk mail to be recycled.

The phone started ringing. Clients were happy to know I had made it through and were still available. Some had been planning projects or were talking with others who were considering a remodel. Just by staying in touch gives a sense of friendship. And friends like to help friends. You can become part of their lives without being annoying. Or could you? Just like those people you hate to see coming to your door, your newsletter could be tossed at first sight. Your widget may be the most exciting thing in your life, but others may not share your passion. I made it a serious point to always give the best I can, and the newsletter wasn't going to be an exception. You know you're doing well when your clients are recommending your newsletter to their friends. Better is when people call because they have been sharing the newsletter from a friend.

After wasting thousands of dollars trying to reach new clients, I'm ashamed for not turning to my past clients first. It's like chasing new friends and ignoring the people that have been part of your life. If you take the time to build good relationships, then don't throw it away just to chase the next dollar.

GIVING YOUR CUSTOMERS THE ROYAL TREATMENT

About John Senska

At a young age John not only built the typical play forts, but complete towns with roads and stores. According to relatives, he had a surprising eye for detail and the relationships between the roads and houses to the toy vehicles he was using. As John grew, his projects also grew. A time or two his parents had to step in and stop the young builder so the fence or some other part of the yard wouldn't end up as part of a current project of his. The cries of needing it for a finishing touch usually fell on deaf ears.

When he was 8 years old, part of his dreams came true. After purchasing a new home, his parents were having remodeling done before they moved in. Walls coming down, the smell of cutting new wood, the new look of an old space all part of what he imagined. John had found the perfect world... until his father started having disagreements with the contractor. Day after day his father's dissatisfaction at the way the remodel was going grew. Like all kids his age, always looking for approval, John couldn't understand how anyone could disappoint someone else. This proved to be a major event to shape John's young mind.

Years later, after graduating from school, John listened to his parents and worked from manufacturing to an office on San Diego Bay. According to his parents these were real jobs, unlike construction. Going from job to job, work became unbearable and draining. While in San Diego, an opportunity to work with a local builder came up. Feeling unsatisfied up to now, John took the job. The first day, coming home dirty, covered in sweat and hurting from every muscle in his body, with a smile, John now knew his future.

That was over twenty years ago. Never forgetting that first lesson he experienced with his Dad, combined with the best that other contractors have taught him, John now owns **John Senska and Sons, Inc.** He believes people deserve to be satisfied with every aspect of a project, even if they don't understand why. This all may be a dream of a child, correcting the disappointment of his father, but it became more: A mission to change back the attitude towards general contractors to a trusted adviser.

Website	www.SenskaAndSons.com
E-Mail	JSenska@SenskaAndSons.com
Phone	847-293-2699 (Please leave a message due to the fact I'm not often in a position to answer my phone, i.e. hanging on a ladder or using a saw)
Fax	847-663-1559 (for those of us old timers)

Check out John's bonus offer:

> **Bonus:**
>
> As a gift for taking the time to read this chapter, I would like to send a *free* copy of my newsletter,
>
> *Elite Homeowner's Monthly*
>
> to help you see how easy it is to stay in touch.
>
> Just contact me at
>
> ## JSenska@SenskaAndSons.com

Chapter 10

To Err Is Human;
To Really Mess Things Up Takes A Computer!

By Robert Bilger

It's the relationship you spend more time on than any other. It deepens every year. And when things go wrong, you become afraid, tearful, and in some cases so enraged that you lash out by throwing things—but you're willing to go right back into the relationship no matter what happens.

What are we talking about? The bond you have with your computer. If you work in an office, chances are you spend more time staring into your computer screen than having conversations with real live human beings. And you probably spend more time at your PC than you do with your significant other, best friend, and even your kids.

According to research conducted by SupportSoft Inc., a firm in Redwood City, California that makes software for computer help desks, people are spending an increasing amount of time at their computer. This survey also revealed how computer problems can unleash powerful—even dangerous emotions. When confronted with a dead computer, 19% admitted to wanting to hurl it out the nearest window, 9% felt stranded and alone, 11% used language normally reserved for special occasions, 7% did so loudly, 3% did so tearfully and another 3% vented their wrath on inanimate objects.

With these results it should come as no surprise that 48% said they would rather help a friend move than deal with a computer problem, and 30% said they felt more frustration with their computer now than in previous years.

GIVING YOUR CUSTOMERS THE ROYAL TREATMENT

Want to have a healthy relationship with your computer? Then start by taking care of it. Two of the main items that most people ignore are their Security and Back Up. Why? Because we all think that we are safe from computer problems happening to us. Most people don't realize that viruses can sneak in anytime they want.

Have you had your child or his/her friends surfing on the family computer? How many times have they gone to a website that they're not supposed to, or downloaded illegal music? Have you checked your employee's computers lately to see if anyone is downloading porn after hours? Back doors open up, and viruses walk in.

I can't tell you how many times I have heard from my clients how they are just getting ready to do a presentation when all of a sudden they lose their file. Timing is coincidental all the time.

And don't think that because your computer is new that you can't have issues. Just because you can't touch or see them, things do lurk in the background. Out of sight, out of mind. Right?

Are You Using Protection?....It's Important!

Recently we have seen a spike in the number of people who have viruses, so here are a few ways that you can stay protected:

1) **It Is A NECESSITY** – If you have a computer, it is very important for you to have an anti-virus program on your computer. Remember that *everything* is important on your computer. Not having an anti-virus could end up costing you more than if you were to pay the yearly subscription for one. It can become costly to remove a

virus. If you don't know how to do this on your own, you will probably have to pay an IT person to do it for you, so that bill could add up. There is also a chance that you could end up losing the information that you have on your computer. Depending on the virus, your computer may have to be reformatted. If that happens it's possible that you will lose your documents, pictures, movies, music, etc.

2) **Keep It Up-To-Date** – There are always new viruses popping up online. Keeping your anti-virus's database updated will help you protect yourself from the new ones that are out there. Check for updates regularly in order to have the best protection your anti-virus will provide. Luckily most of them stay up to date automatically, but it is important to check on that periodically.

3) **Free vs. Paid**- There are pros and cons to the free vs paid anti-virus programs.
    A. Retail Anti-Virus Programs
        1. Offer more features (i.e. Email scans, Parental controls, Identity theft protection, spyware / malware protection, etc.)
        2. A free anti-virus typically will not offer technical support
        3. A free anti-virus will usually have ads
        4. Free anti-viruses don't always detect viruses as well as paid ones
        5. Free anti-viruses don't do as well at removing viruses as the paid ones
        6. Most free anti-viruses take longer to scan your system
    B. Free Anti-Virus Programs
        1. .....It's FREE

GIVING YOUR CUSTOMERS THE ROYAL TREATMENT

      2. Your subscription doesn't end and you can always update the database
      3. Free Anti-Virus programs typically don't scan for Spyware / Malware.
      4. Most paid anti-viruses need to be renewed in order to update the database for new viruses (paid yearly)

4) **Run It** – Always be sure that your anti-virus is running regularly. Either schedule it to run or open it up and run the scans once a week. Just like when you are getting sick, if you find a virus early enough, you may be able to stop it before it infects your whole system.

5) **Not Everything Is a Virus** – When your anti-virus runs, it is possible that it will find files that aren't necessarily a virus, but it may look suspicious. Don't panic; just follow the steps your anti-virus uses to remove/neutralize it.

6) **Use Only One** – Only use one anti-virus. If you have more than one, you can run into issues where they fight against each other and just stop working, or they can end up blocking you from being able to get on to the internet at all.

This is not an exhaustive list, just a quick discussion on advantages of using a Full Anti-Virus program versus a free one. But more importantly, you need something on your computer to help protect you. According to the latest Internet Security report, over 10,000 computers become infected every day because they are not properly protected or maintained.

Let's Back It Up!

We need it, and we rely on it. Anyone that uses a computer should use some form of it. What I'm talking about is called data back-up. Without it could be the difference between a slight computer setback, or living through your own electronic apocalypse.

Let's get real. In this day and age our computers are a part of our lives. We work on them, we play on them, we shop on them, and we keep in touch with friends and family on them. They've replaced telephone books, encyclopedias, stereos, and yes, even the mailman. They've become ledgers, journals, and photo albums.

But contrary to popular belief, computers are not perfect. Motherboards malfunction, files become corrupt and CPU's call it quits, taking our precious data with them. There's no question about it, it just happens. If you use your computer long enough, it or the parts inside of it will fail at some point. The worst thing that can happen is that the hard drive fails. On a complete failure of a hard drive, that may mean the data is not recoverable. Hence the reason every magazine article and newspaper tip tells you to **Back-up, Back-up and then Back-up**.

So take that as a good idea to keep all of your data backed up, or at least the important stuff that you don't want to lose. Recently we have seen a few failed hard drives. Some of them we have been able to recover information and some of them we were not able to. Don't think that your computer is too new for yours to fail, either. We saw one that was still under warranty so they sent it back to the manufacturer. Hard drives have a lot of moving and sensitive parts, and if they are bumped around a lot or hard enough, they can start to have errors.

So the best defense is backing up your system.

Backing up data is imperative for businesses. Lost information can cause a major crisis, or possibly even business failure. While

GIVING YOUR CUSTOMERS THE ROYAL TREATMENT

an individual may not risk financial ruin, it can certainly be frustrating, and even heartbreaking.

There are so many back-up programs that are completely automatic and will save your precious data, including all those great pictures of your grandchildren!

Quick Summary of Tips

1) Always make sure your computer is up to date with Windows Updates and Security patches. It can save you untold headaches.
2) Schedule routine maintenance by an IT professional to keep your system(s) running good. Some preventative work can save you hours and keep everything running smooth. Think of it like your car: take care of it and it will take care of you.
3) Always remember to back-up your important files regularly. The short amount of time it takes will save you hours of time trying to recreate that payroll spreadsheet or the last big order that was rushed in at the last minute. Or better yet, get with your favorite IT guy or gal and get a regular / automatic Back-up program going and let it do ALL the work!

So remember, to keep your computer running smoothly, keep your anti-virus up to date, and stay away from websites that are misleading.

ROBERT BILGER

About Robert Bilger

Robert Bilger is the owner/operator of PC Medics of Wisconsin, LLC., which provides computer & technical consulting to local small businesses, as well as home PC users. His goal is to set the standard for on-site computer solutions through fast, outstanding service & response. PC Medics customers will always receive one-on-one personal attention by focusing on the customer first, and their technology issues second.

After serving in the U.S. Navy for 7 years, Robert started helping people with computers. In 1998 he opened PC Medics of Wisconsin, LLC. which serves the Milwaukee and Chicago areas, to help people keep their businesses on track with healthy computers. He loves to develop relationships with his clients, and the computer challenges they bring are just a bonus!

Robert enjoys his free time with his wife Darice and their 2 daughters.

For more information on Robert's services, visit his website at **www.RobsPCMedics.com,** or contact him directly at 262-620-

GIVING YOUR CUSTOMERS THE ROYAL TREATMENT

1040 or **Support@RobsPCMedics.com.**

SPECIAL OFFER

Need computer help or your problems fixed? Need technical consultation on what to do next? We have a special offer for those that have taken advantage of reading this book.

Call us at **262-620-1040** and request a *FREE 2 Hour Consultation* by mentioning the **CODE "Problem Free"**

Why are we offering this?
People need help with technical problems and what better way to get to know us then by showing up and helping you with your computer / technical problems.

You can use the 2 Hours any way you want.

A limit of 1 Free consultation per customer, please.

Chapter 11

5 Secrets to Being Super Productive, Implementing More of Your Ideas, and Building Your Business Faster

The *BUILD* Success System

By Ronald Guzik

ALL SMALL BUSINESS OWNERS want to get more done. They want to put into practice more of their best business-building ideas, build their business faster and better, and be more successful. However, things get in the way. Snags and glitches and daunting day-by-day challenges seem to hold back your well-thought-out plans to boost your productivity. You know what you want to do, but you just can't get it done. It may seem like the classic one step forward, two steps back.

For many years I myself struggled with just this quandary in my previous business projects. Finally I decided that I would search out the most effective leading-edge techniques for becoming more productive so that I could implement more of my ideas, and be more successful.

What I learned over time goes far beyond your standard time-management tips for making "To Do" lists and setting priorities. I learned, in effect, the underlying or real reasons that people in business lag far behind the productivity and success that they are hoping for.

Here are the Five Secrets that I discovered. As an ensemble, I call this the *B U I L D* Success System:

GIVING YOUR CUSTOMERS THE ROYAL TREATMENT

Believe That You Can Get Better

This is probably the simplest, but most overlooked secret to success. To get better you first have to believe you can do it. This is especially true in the areas where you struggle the most, with the things that most hold you back.

Without this important belief you'll stay stuck in your current level of skill or expertise.

When you finally believe you can get better and take action to sharpen your skills—in whatever area, time management (e.g., procrastination), people management, financial management, marketing, etc. -- that's when you'll break through to genuine progress.

Carol Dweck, in her book *Mindsets: The New Psychology of Success,* calls this "the Growth Mindset versus the Fixed Mindset." The Fixed Mindset tells you "your weaknesses are set in stone and cannot be changed." The Growth Mindset says, "No! You can learn and you can get better."

"The growth mindset," she writes, "is based on the belief that...everyone can change and grow through application and experience." A much healthier way to think.

How to start to make this switch?

To acquire what I like to call the "I can get better" mindset, start by noticing if you actually believe you can become more productive and better at implementation, or if you have been telling yourself "I'm just not good at that" (whatever "that" is).

Next, recall areas of your life where you started out with minimal or weak skills, and yet you learned. Perhaps you were a major procrastinator but now, after some deliberate steps, you've found that you can indeed take action when you need to do so.

Or maybe you once felt you could not speak in front of a group of people to save your life. You'd rather have had a root canal done with no Novocain than give a speech. But then, slowly, you started giving talks to a few people and worked your way up to being able to handle yourself in front of larger groups.

Or again, perhaps you felt out of place at networking events. Gradually, however, you came up with a pretty good "elevator speech," practiced it at home or with a friend or mate, and learned to effectively work a room.

By reminding yourself that in certain areas you started with weak skills but over time got better, you will reinforce the "I can get better" or growth mindset.

Uncover Your Limiting Mental Models

Your mental models, or beliefs, are your internal maps of the world. They define what is possible. They guide your day-to-day behaviors. They either support increasing productivity through implementation of your best ideas, or they hinder this effort.

Instead of trying to argue with yourself over whether your current beliefs are "true" or not, learn to assess whether they are holding you back from achieving your goals, or supporting you in reaching those goals.

Realize that your mental models guide all of your decisions and actions. They shape your belief about what is possible for you to achieve. To move beyond your current rate of improvement you have to change the picture of what you believe is possible. Otherwise, you won't even try to improve, or at best you'll make only a half-hearted effort.

Take, for instance, an attitude toward money. Typical beliefs include these: It takes hard work to make money. Rich people are bad because they got where they are through greed. It takes money to make money. Or maybe even "Money is the root of all evil." This last is a misquote from the Bible. The actual verse says *"The **love** of money is the root of all evil."*
(1 Timothy 6:10).

Your mental models are often unconscious. For instance, you don't go around saying "It takes hard work to make money;" however, your actions show that is what you believe.

You learned most of your mental models as a child. You heard them from parents or uncles or teachers. A racial prejudice is an example.

By tuning in to your "self-talk" you will be able to uncover your mental models or beliefs. Then they will be "out there" for you to inspect—and judge. Remember: You can only change what you can uncover and examine. This is what Socrates meant when he said, "The unexamined life is not worth living," (from Plato's *Apology*).

*I*mprove Your Emotional Resiliency

Emotional resiliency is the key to implementing change strategies to achieve super productivity.

This is the "bounce back" skill. It's the basis for staying

motivated, getting things done, and working well with people.

We all know how a bad moment or a bad day can throw us completely off track. You lose motivation and you drag in taking the actions you know you need to reach your goals.

Emotional resiliency will help you cut through your negative feelings and get your day or your week back on track.

This technique relies on overall "emotional intelligence," as it is often called. It includes self-awareness, self-motivation, the capacity to manage your feelings and your reactions to others' comments and behaviors.

When the winds of adversity blow down hard, you will be better able to withstand the storms. And bounce back. That means you'll get back more quickly to working toward your goals. You won't stay stuck in gloom and doom.

Let's say your company has a contract to provide a service, such as painting an entire apartment complex. You've asked for a deposit of 30 per cent on the job. That deposit will allow you to buy all the materials you'll need without borrowing from the bank. But the client says no—nothing down, all payments will be made when the work is finished. A big blow.

If your emotional resiliency is working for you, you'll be able to get through your initial downbeat reaction and figure out what to do. Perhaps if the client's payment track record is good, you'll decide to front the materials and "keep truckin'." Or give up the job and aggressively seek another contract in town. And feel OK about it either way.

Once you can identify your feelings, it will be easier to release them. So focus your attention on what's going on inside of you:

GIVING YOUR CUSTOMERS THE ROYAL TREATMENT

Are you feeling sad, disappointed, annoyed, angry, or anxious and afraid? (Or some combination of these?)

Personally, I like to focus my attention on my body's sensations and breathe into that part of my body (head, heart, abdomen, etc.). I visualize the negative feeling leaving my body and I feel better. (For a more detailed description of this technique, see *The Sedona Method* by Hale Dwoskin).

Other ways to develop better emotional skills are through journaling, sharing feelings with others and working through programs such as Marshall Rosenberg's *Non-Violent Communication*.

Look Forward Toward Your Goals

Here I am talking about the kind of focused intention that will keep you on track and moving toward your goals. By focusing your intention on what you want in life instead of on what you don't want (i.e., your current problems), you'll improve your chances of reaching your goals.

Many of us spend a whole lot of time talking about how our lives are not what we want. This seems natural and normal. And it does take quite an effort to shift our focus away from the negatives and toward the best outcomes we desire for ourselves, our family, and our work life.

Try this: Draw a circle on a sheet of paper. Next draw a line down the center. Write on the left side all the things that are not so great in your life. Write on the right side all the things that you're happy about.

Cover the right side with an opaque sheet of paper so that only the left side—the negative—is visible. How does looking at just that side make you feel?

Now cover the left side in the same way and focus your attention just on the positives. And see how you feel. Quite a different feeling, isn't it?

Wouldn't it make sense to put most of your energy and focus into seeing the positives? Wouldn't that help you cope better with the negatives, rather than putting all your energy into *focusing* on those negatives?

After this experiment, watch yourself day by day. See where you are focusing most of your energy. Is it on the positives in your life? Or on the negatives? Consciously decide that you will spend more time focusing on the positives—and celebrating them. You'll soon be convinced that it's the positive focus, rather than the negative focus, that will truly move you down the track toward your goals.

*D*elight in Your Progress

Along your journey to success there can indeed be many obstacles to overcome. Bashing away at these obstacles can sap your energy and your motivation. That is why it is especially important to delight in your progress and your accomplishments. Cultivating the simple habit of finding satisfaction in your progress will boost your morale, increase your motivation and move you forward toward success.

So delight in the journey. Celebrate every bit of progress along the way.

In other words, be happy NOW. Don't fall for the illusion that

GIVING YOUR CUSTOMERS THE ROYAL TREATMENT

you'll only be happy "after I am finally successful." That's a bear trap.

Harvard professor Shawn Akin, in his book *The Happiness Advantage,* shares research that shows that most people have the formula wrong. The majority think that happiness will come to them when they become successful.

> "Conventional wisdom holds," Akin writes, "that if we work hard, we will be more successful, and if we are more successful, *then* we'll be happy. If we can just find that great job, win that next promotion and lose those five pounds, happiness will follow.
>
> But recent discoveries in the field of positive psychology have shown that this formula is actually backward.
>
> Happiness fuels success, not the other way around.
>
> When we are positive, our brains become more engaged, creative, motivated, energetic, resilient, and productive at work. This isn't just an empty mantra. This discovery has been repeatedly borne out by rigorous research in psychology and neuroscience, management studies, and the bottom line of organizations around the globe."

A version of this "delighting in your progress" step is taught in virtually every management system today, but few people actually grab onto it and do it. Somehow we skip the step of "feeling grateful" or "giving thanks" or "celebrating the small successes." Don't short change yourself. Do the step.

Celebrate a bit when you cross off key items on your "To Do" list. Tell yourself, even out loud if you can, "Good work!" "Great job!" Stop being one of those people who simply move on to the next item without realizing that they've accomplished something worthwhile. Doing so will mean you'll actually lose, rather than gain, the energy you need to knock aside the next obstacle in your path.

Delight in your progress! And feel good about yourself.

The *BUILD* Success System works. You want to:

> *B*elieve You Can Get Better
>
> *U*ncover Your Limiting Mental Models (Beliefs)
>
> *I*mprove Your Emotional Resiliency
>
> *L*ook Forward Toward Your Goals
>
> *D*elight in Your Progress

That's the path to putting your best ideas into action, increasing your productivity, building your business faster—and tasting success.

GIVING YOUR CUSTOMERS THE ROYAL TREATMENT

About Ronald Guzik

Ronald Guzik, the principal at Guzik Business Development, helps small business owners implement more of their business-building ideas and strategies so they can grow their businesses faster and achieve their goals.

He is a seasoned entrepreneur, business consultant, productivity coach, master trainer, and small business author with over 30 years of business experience. He has been a management consultant working with small businesses, VP of a start-up finance company which grew to $60 million annual revenues, Senior Accountant doing consulting projects, and computer consultant designing customer software for small businesses.

As a small business consultant Mr. Guzik helped a specialty retail store grow 80% in six months using marketing programs and business systems enhancements. He provided personal productivity coaching to a real estate agent and helped her double her sales in one year.

Ron has taught, designed and led business development workshops on strategic planning, sales, marketing, finance, accounting and management, and professional development programs on time management, people skills, communication skills, conflict resolution and personal change. When he taught at Harper College's Small Business Development Center he received the highest rating from students' reviews ever seen at the Center.

Ron is the author of *Build Your Business Stronger and Do it Quickly!* and *The Inner Game of Entrepreneuring*. He has been quoted in *Entrepreneur*, *Business Start-Up* and *Black Enterprise* magazines, and has appeared on many radio and TV programs, including Wisdom TV.

BONUS # 1

For a *Free Webinar* on

The **5 Secrets to Being Super Productive, Implementing More of Your Ideas, and Building Your Business Faster**,

go to

ImplementYourIdeas.com

BONUS # 2

Register to win one of several **Incredible Bonuses,** including:

- One *Free half-hour individual one-on-one Implementation Skills Coaching* call to get personal feedback on your implementation skills and ways to improve them. ($125 value, Limit 10)

- One *Free* **Guzik Ultimate Entrepreneur Success System**™ home study course based on the book *Build Your Business Stronger.* This includes a comprehensive Business Review and Analysis for people who are feeling stuck with slow or no growth. ($197 value, Limit 2)

- **Grand Prize**: *One Month Free of the* **Turbo Charge Your Marketing and Implement Your Ideas Complete Consulting and Coaching Package.** Experience the powerful business-building combination of improving your marketing and enhancing your implementation skills to turbo-charge your growth. ($700 value, Limit 1)

Register Today at

ImplementYourIdeas.com/bookoffer

Bonus # 3
($97 value)

Would you like to implement more of your business building ideas?

Discover your **Implementation Skills Quotient (ISQ).**

Take Ron Guzik's
Free Implementation Skills Assessment
and find out what is holding you back from implementing more of your business ideas.
Get Yours Today at

ImplementYourIdeas.com/bookoffer

For your questions, comments or feedback on the chapter, I can be reached at:
Ronald Guzik
P.O. Box 87711
Carol Stream, IL 60188-7711
Ron@Build-Your-Business-Stronger.com
630-605-5111

GIVING YOUR CUSTOMERS THE ROYAL TREATMENT

"I'M SUCCESSFUL AT MY HOBBY AND MY BUSINESS, THANKS TO ACE LUCIANO!"

Chapter 12

Success "Secrets" for Sales and Business

By Jerry "Ace"Luciano

How to be successful, regardless of your industry

You know, I'm often asked for the "Secret" to success in business.

It is second only to, "I want to do what you do for a living and work in the outdoor industry."

The secret is, THERE REALLY IS NO SECRET.

The problem is that most people just aren't willing to put in the time, dedication, money, and small sacrifices now in order to have all the time, lots of money, and massive benefits and rewards in the future.

There are, however, certain things that can make it easier along the way.

Here are a few tips that have helped me become who I am today, and hopefully they will help you in your success, also:

> 1) **FIND A MENTOR OR COACH**...One of the clearest and easiest pieces of advice that came from one of my favorite books on success, "Think and Grow Rich," by Napoleon Hill. It is so much easier to learn from other's mistakes instead of wasting time making them on your own!
>
> 2) **Do what you say you're going to do when you say you're going to do it.** I'm amazed at how much of my

GIVING YOUR CUSTOMERS THE ROYAL TREATMENT

business has been built just by coming through on my word.

3) **Work smart.** If you want to be an entrepreneur or successful salesperson you have to make time for things through leverage. Your time is valuable, so pay someone else to do tasks that aren't worth your rate.

4) **Always give and give and give before you ask for anything.** People don't trust sales people. If you want to be successful in sales you have to (1) prove that you are very different and (2) you are there for the customers' benefit and the customer alone. Provide lots of value.

5) **Keep your ratio in order.** God gave you 2 ears and 1 mouth for a reason. I've found that I've sold much more by listening than talking.

6) **Forget what you think your business is.** Whether a dentist, doctor, lawyer, salesperson, plumber, or restaurant owner, your business is SELLING your BUSINESS, therefore, your BUSINESS is SALES!

7) **Follow the 80-20 rule.** Do not get bogged down by the 80% of the people that can be a complete waste of your time. Focus on the 20% that make you money, but also make happy those people that are on the lower end of the spectrum. I've made a lot of money servicing people that were ignored... and they were ignored because people thought they were "too small" or not worth their time. Well, I've taken on a bunch of those people and made several of them into millionaires.

I learned these tips over a long and circuitous path to success. You don't have to...but more on that later.

I feel like I have an "unfair advantage" compared to some, as I was blessed with hard-working, self-sacrificing parents that did everything in their power to instill in me a can-do attitude and relentless work ethic.

You may not be so fortunate, but that doesn't mean that you can't overcome any obstacles in your path.

The Circuitous Path...

Oddly enough, I never wanted to be in sales.

Pretty odd, considering that I was raised in a family in which my father was an entrepreneur and businessman. It was a hard life sometimes, but also had its rewards, as my family was able to travel, hunt, and fish all over the globe. My parents just wanted different for me...

From the time I was 7 years old, I was destined by my parents to become a doctor. Other family members and family friends were in the medical field, there was a lot of money attached to becoming a doctor, and they all had very successful lives, big, beautiful houses, and what seemed like really great lives, so that was my path. For the next 15 years I ran with it. I studied my way through high school, I went all the way through college as a pre-med major, and even tried to apply to medical school (unceremoniously rejected), then applied to Physician Assistant school, then applied to Physical Therapy school, and I couldn't get into any of them. My grades were good...just not quite good enough.

I Land a "DREAM JOB"

After several years of working 2-3 part-time jobs while still trying to get into medical school, I actually became a Pharmaceutical Sales Representative- one of the most highly-coveted sales positions out there at the time. At that time you needed both a medical background AND sales experience. Now,

GIVING YOUR CUSTOMERS THE ROYAL TREATMENT

I had learned how to sell in an unusual way- by being thrown into it! You see, my father had a heart attack when I was 16 and was hospitalized for several weeks while doctors tried to determine what was wrong. My mother and sisters had no knowledge of our family construction business, so I was thrust into a position of leadership by default. In the morning, I would start my father's construction crews, show up late to first period at school, then in the afternoon run leads and bid and sell more jobs. Thanks to my family work ethic and a very understanding Catholic high school, I not only held things together, but made some serious money! I also had to work smart and leverage my time, or there was no way it was all going to hold together. It was clearly a baptism by fire- but I not only survived, but thrived.

So here I was, in a "dream job" in the Upper Peninsula of Michigan, working as a Pharma Rep for 8 years and winning major award after major award after major award, all while making a FANTASTIC living. Using the principles outlined at the beginning of this chapter, I took a territory that was literally the bottom of the basement of all the territories in the division, and in 18 months I was able to take it to one of the top performing territories in the country. My wife and I went on trips to exotic places like Australia and Mexico. I was able to "make it happen" mostly because I treated all of my customers the way I was taught to treat them- I provided <u>value</u> to my customers, and I treated them the way I wanted to be treated- by respecting their time, discussing and focusing on THEIR goals, and making them money.

That was my first long-term experience reflecting that when you give MASSIVE amounts of value to a customer and a prospect before you ask for anything in return, it pays you back in spades. It was also here that one of my dear friends and mentors, Joe Christiansen, instilled in me tip #4- "Keep your ratio in order."

My wife and I built both our home and family "up north," settling on a parcel of paradise in Marquette, Michigan. Life was really, really good.

Unfortunately, due to massive abuses by several companies, their sales managers, and their representatives (I will never forget being told that I "had to spend more money or the region would lose it"), that industry dropped off of a cliff in 2005. Why did that happen, and happen so quickly? CUSTOMER ABUSE!

Companies overflowed territories with sales reps. At one point I was selling the exact same products as four other representatives in my territory selling to the same doctors. Every four to five days the doctors were seeing all of us. Eventually, the doctors stopped seeing reps, even good ones. Not surprisingly, this action was followed by massive layoffs, and even though I was a top producer, I also got my pink slip. The dream life we had built shattered, and due to the lack of comparable jobs we had to leave.

A Door Opens…

…Because I pushed it hard and steadily, then stuck my foot through!

Foolishly, I tried to stay in the pharmaceutical industry, competing for every job with 6,000 other layoff victims and new graduate hopefuls willing to do ANYTHING to "get a foot in the door" for less positions that were paying less and less money.

To help make ends meet I was doing some consulting work. I had several opportunities presented to me in several industries,

GIVING YOUR CUSTOMERS THE ROYAL TREATMENT

but I thought, "If I'm going to sell something, I should sell something that I'm passionate about. I'm a passionate hunter, fisherman, and outdoorsman, and someone has to sell that stuff." So for the better part of six or seven months I networked and talked with people, attended the national trade shows at my own expense, went to every hunters convention and show, bought hundreds of rounds of drinks and more than a few lunches and dinners, and talked with everyone, including dozens of HR people. I found out the hard way that every position in the outdoor industry is coveted. People rarely leave, and when they do there are dozens of direct referrals in line to be hired before those positions are even advertised as open.

Good for them...bad for me.

Two "Lucky Breaks..."

"Break #1"...I can't help but laugh a little bit when people say I am "lucky." I can assure you that luck had very little to do with it. It was more like finishing the first leg in a multi-part race. I met one person, who referred me to another person, who then referred me to another. That final person was Scott Dobry of H & G Marketing, who became both a mentor and friend to me to this day. At his company they had no room for any more sales people, but they did need a "Pro Staffer." Sales representatives in the outdoor industry have LARGE geographies to cover. They can't possibly be everywhere they have to be. A Pro Staffer fills in at events that the sales rep couldn't cover. I was good at it, and generally sold out of all my products. I worked some events, met some people, and then in 2007 I competed in the "Field and Stream Total Outdoorsman Challenge," a nation-wide contest that was televised. This led to Bass Pro Shops offering me a local hunting pro position in the Gurnee, Illinois store for their Redhead Hunting Apparel.

JERRY "ACE" LUCIANO

Break #2… The job that nobody, including me, respected, but launched me to success…

I needed to make more money, as consulting and pro-staffing wasn't doing enough for me. I was referred into a position selling…YELLOW PAGES.

I know.

The guy every business hates (including my own father!) The slick, fast-talking salesman that swaggers in, driving a high-end car and somehow manages to talk you into spending more money that you did the year before because, after all, how will people find your business? I signed on because they told me that if I wanted more money, then all I had to do was sell more. No one in my professional life had ever told me this before. That just didn't happen in the pharmaceutical world. There were years when I sold a LOT more, yet made the same or even LESS!

Training was downtown Chicago for a MONTH. Since I hate the city, I threw myself into my work…planning, preparing, and studying, to the position of #1 in the training class. It was actually easy, because I knew what I hated, told my story of a small businessman that hated Yellow Page reps, actually did my best for each client, and built a literal mob of raving fans that referred me to new account after new account. Before I hit the field, a manager told me "you should talk to this guy that is also out in the field; he's a lot like you, and his name is Steve Sipress." They specifically singled me out because I was smashing all the records that Steve made the year before. It was clearly one of the only times luck had really played a roll. Steve was a sales and marketing machine; we were cut from the same cloth, and he and I are great friends to this day.

GIVING YOUR CUSTOMERS THE ROYAL TREATMENT

I sold Yellow Pages for several years, and when people asked me how I was able to make any money, they were surprised when I told them that not only did I have a "top-5% income," I was actually promoted to the highest sales level in the Yellow Pages faster than any other rep before or since. I promoted myself...TWICE...through my account-building success and became an Account Manager.

The truth is, I would have stayed at the Yellow Pages for a long time, but they did not get on board right away with the internet. They were "victims of their own hubris," in that they did what was best for them, not the customer, and the customers made them pay...dearly! The company went bankrupt, cut our pay in half, and I knew it was time to move on, but all the while, I never lost sight of my goal of a successful outdoor industry career.

Oddly enough, I didn't start looking for another job. Because of my performance, jobs were approaching me. I was being called by dozens of headhunters. Going back to my medical roots, I took a job selling defibrillators and resuscitation equipment to hospitals. My "claim to fame" there was that I converted one of the largest Health Care systems in the US... *after* they already signed with another company. But once again, this company had serious issues; great products, but lots of pressure. In the horrible economy of 2008-2010, hospitals were just not spending money if they didn't have to. It didn't matter what we did or said. At the end of our 3rd quarter, we were 26% to our goals. Layoffs ensued, and since the company had a multi-million dollar contract now whether I was there or not, that included me.

I then sold for a Fortune 500 company doing Internet Marketing and Advertising for Attorneys, again in a territory that nobody had ever done anything with. By being entirely different, offering MASSIVE value, creating a raving mob of enthusiastic fans, and also living tip #6, I broke all the compensation records for my territory two years in a row, and was well on my way again when I decided that it was time to move on.

Over my career, and regardless of the industries that I was in, regardless of what I sold or didn't sell, I have always been on top of my game.

My business, like all of my customers and businesses that I have consulted with, is sales!

From Indoors to Outdoors

All the while I had been taking time off of work to attend trade shows, worked events over weekends, and networked like a madman. I spent an hour a day giving value to my contacts and group on LinkedIn, and I basically built my business from scratch. I saw that there was a gaping hole in the industry, that there were companies looking for what I did, and I knew I could do it. I knew there was a need for several services, and I bet that if I picked up a few different companies I could have consistent work for these trade events. I knew that if I provided massive value and built my own pipeline, I could have my own successful business.

So that's what I did.

I've sold everything in the outdoor world from optics to firearms to ammunition to mineral supplements to broad heads and arrows...pretty much you name it, and I've handled it, touched it, sold it, and pushed it somehow, somewhere, sometime.

Being a little smarter than the average bear, I've always

GIVING YOUR CUSTOMERS THE ROYAL TREATMENT

preferred to learn from other's mistakes, instead of making a bunch of my own. So I talked to everybody, and I built up a very extensive network of outdoor professionals, which has since become the largest network of its kind. It's a group called "Hunting, Fishing and Outdoor Professionals." It's a place for people to exchange their ideas; a large mastermind group where people ask questions and have them answered by some of the top people around.

Also, knowing that I could learn a lot from people that have done and built businesses before, I hired a coach. That coach was Steve Sipress, who has motivated me, instructed me, and inspired me to the tune of several Million Dollars.

Bit by bit I built my business up. I became a VP of sales for a company. I continued to be a constant "student of the sale" and "marketing disciple," meeting with and networking with some of the top people in the industry all over the world. Consequently I have built my own multiple-branched business in the outdoor arena. Now I advise companies big and small, as well as individual businesses based on application, with sales and marketing. Sometimes I represent them at shows, sometimes I direct sell their products, and sometimes I'm just the compensated face of their product.

My Company started as an idea from my "hobby" and makes a "top 10%" level income... doing something that I love to do! I advise people on how to market, sell, and build their own businesses; I've even made several millionaires, with more on their way.

The company is BGA Enterprises, LLC. It consists of a Marketing arm, a Trade Show arm, a Sales Agency arm, a Booking Agency, and a Consulting and Coaching program. My websites, www.AceLuciano.com, www.BigGameAce.com, and www.WorldGameHunts.com have become highly-rated sources of both information and revenue.

I suppose in that sense, I'm really lucky.

I send people on their dream trips all over the world, regardless of their income. I'm very good at inspiring people and helping them achieve their goals. I've been so fortunate to do what I do. I've traveled the world over. I've hunted, fished, and travelled all over four continents. I've been to Africa on safari four times already, and going on my fifth trip next year. I travel frequently, often with my family. I was brought up in life and business knowing that all of these things are available to do, and that you just had to set your mind to it.

My father always said: "If you say you can't, you won't."

I "woke up" one day, said "I CAN!" and you can, too!

GIVING YOUR CUSTOMERS THE ROYAL TREATMENT

About Jerry "Ace" Luciano

Ace has two "secret identities," depending on who you ask. If you ask people in the Executive world, Ace is a "suit and tie wearing executive level sales & marketing professional that likes to hunt and fish."

If you ask someone in the OUTDOOR world, Ace is a "camouflage shirt-wearing hunter, fisherman and gonzo sales and marketing person."

...and Ace does it all because he got tired of waiting for someone else to make a decision about his future.

Ace is first a Hunter, a fisherman, and an outdoorsman for over 30+ years. He is also an author, seminar speaker, consultant, husband, father, and entrepreneur.

Ace has traveled the globe in pursuit of both game and fish throughout the United States, Canada, Mexico, Africa, Europe, and Australia and is involved in numerous conservation organizations and youth projects.

In 1995 Ace became the youngest director ever elected to the board of directors of any Safari Club International chapter. The

JERRY "ACE" LUCIANO

Chapters that he has helped to found have earned Rookie Chapter of the Year, Chapter of the Year, and Conservation Organization of the Year honors.

In 2007, Ace was a finalist in the second ever <u>Field and Stream</u> Total Outdoorsman Challenge, leading to his discovery by <u>Bass Pro</u>, and subsequent invitation to join their pro staff. Ace now lends his sales and marketing talents to numerous outdoor companies as both a Pro Staff Member and a sales and marketing consultant. Most recently Ace has been spending time pursuing his passion of introducing youths to the outdoors through the <u>United Sportsman's Youth Foundation,</u> and writing articles and providing live coverage and commentary for several media outlets.

Ace's highly successful booking agency, World Game Hunts, Ltd., specializes in affordable and unbelievable hunting and fishing trips for all budgets. If you think you can't afford to go on that trip of a lifetime, contact **Ace.**

Most recently, and due to proven methods and systems, Ace was honored by both Mossy Oak and Remington as the number one Mossy Oak pro-staffer out of over 1,100 nationwide... THREE YEARS IN A ROW!

As a 20 year veteran of sales and marketing, Ace has won the

GIVING YOUR CUSTOMERS THE ROYAL TREATMENT

pinnacle sales award at every company for which he was employed. This makes Ace uniquely qualified in the industry, and he now lends that expertise to numerous businesses in the outdoor marketplace.

To find out more about Ace, visit his websites at www.AceLuciano.com, www.BigGameAce.com, and www.WorldGameHhunts.com.

Want to LEAP out of the gates with your new business or even RE-VITALIZE your CURRENT business?

Then take advantage of these SPECIAL OFFERS for purchasers of this book:

Bonus # 1

($97 value)

FREE 30 Min

Business Consultation

when you visit

www.AceLuciano.com

and enter the code

"aceconsult30"

Bonus # 2

($397-$797 value)

50% off

Monthly Retainer Fees

when you visit

www.AceLuciano.com

and use the code

"successbook3"

Bonus # 3

Visit

www.BigGameAce.com

and request your **FREE REPORT**

"The Three Biggest Mistakes Outdoor Companies Make in Their Business"

GIVING YOUR CUSTOMERS THE ROYAL TREATMENT

"I KNOW I HAVE MOLD SOMEWHERE IN MY HOME – HELP ME, GREG BOWEN!"

Chapter 13

The Ultimate Guide to Mold Removal

By Greg Bowen

Mold – disgusting, smelly, slimy, and gross. Not something you want to discuss in polite company. Yet mold is a fact of life. It can be found in almost every environment, outdoors and in. Tiny mold spores, invisible to the naked eye, are entering your home each time you open your front door on a breezy day. But that doesn't mean it's time to don the hazmat suit as you go about your daily chores.

It's important to understand that mold isn't necessarily bad. In fact, it's an important part of nature's recycling program, speeding along the decomposition process of fallen leaves, branches, and other dead plant materials. And don't forget about blue cheese and antibiotics. But elevated levels of mold in your home or workplace, where it doesn't belong, can be harmful and should be treated by a professional mold remediator.

What Causes Indoor Mold Problems?

Mold reproduces by creating microscopic spores that travel through the air, much like a dandelion creates airborne seeds. The spores are so small and light that they can travel great distances, blowing into your home through an open window or door. This is why it is impossible to have a home completely free of all mold.

Some mold is normal, but it becomes problematic when the mold indoors starts growing. Mold needs only two things to grow – food and moisture. Unfortunately, most mold isn't

GIVING YOUR CUSTOMERS THE ROYAL TREATMENT

terribly picky about what it eats. It thrives on many building materials, especially those made of cellulose, like wood framing, plywood, and drywall. But even with an abundant supply of food, mold doesn't grow until moisture is added. This is why the most common problem areas are those areas of the home that are damp or humid – attics, basements, crawl spaces, and bathrooms.

The key to preventing indoor mold problems is controlling the moisture. In attics, this generally means correcting improper ventilation or redirecting exhaust fans from bathrooms or a kitchen through the roof instead of into the attic. Controlling moisture in bathrooms can be accomplished by adding or upgrading exhaust fans, or simply making sure that splashes are cleaned up promptly. When water is present in the basement or crawlspace, it's time to consider waterproofing measures – foundation crack repairs, sump pumps, or drain systems. But moisture problems can occur almost anywhere in the home, caused by high humidity, leaks, drips, or condensation. If a Mold Remediation Company proposes to clean up the existing mold without recommending moisture control to prevent future problems, it's time to look elsewhere.

Sometimes the cause of the moisture is a specific event instead of a chronic problem – a burst pipe, an overflowing bathtub, a curious child who decided to see if a window well can be converted into a Barbie swimming pool using a garden hose. It's important that the wet area be dried quickly, as a mold problem can develop as soon as 24-48 hours after the water damage occurs. Although it can be tempting to see if you can save some money by cleaning up a flood yourself instead of hiring a professional, it will end up costing quite a bit more if water damage turns into mold contamination.

Why Be Concerned About Indoor Mold?

Although your indoor environment can't be mold-free, it's important that moisture be controlled to limit the growth. The damaging effects of mold fall into three main categories: structural, financial, and health.

Structural Damage

Mold consumes building materials. Left untreated, the damage can reach the point where the frame supporting your home can become damaged to the extent that the roof, walls, or floors will need to be replaced.

Financial Loss

Mold remediation isn't cheap, especially when it's done right. Steps must be taken not only to remove mold, but to prevent spores from contaminating other areas of the home during the removal process. And many homeowners are dismayed to find that mold remediation isn't typically an expense that is covered by their insurance policy.

Mold also comes in to play when it's time to sell a home. A buyer that hears "mold" may panic, causing the sale to fall through. Even if the transaction doesn't come to a screeching halt as a result of the diagnosis, complications can arise. A well-meaning attorney may add language to the contract, requiring proof that the home is "free of mold", or require that the work be done by a "licensed mold remediator." As it isn't possible to have a home completely free of all traces of mold due to its ubiquitous nature, and most states don't have licensing requirements for mold remediators, the seller will now have the added challenge of renegotiating the contract to appease the potential buyer. In most cases, it's a smart move to have any mold problems resolved by a qualified, certified remediation firm that will warranty their work before putting the home on the market.

Health and Safety

The most important reason to have a mold problem properly rectified is for the health and safety of the occupants. Mold can cause a variety of health issues, and the effects vary from one individual to another.

"Toxic Mold"

Most people have probably heard about so-called "toxic mold" at one time or another. Usually the term refers to a specific species of mold, *Stachybotrys chartarum*, also referred to as "black mold". But mold itself (even *Stachybotrys chartarum*) isn't toxic or poisonous; some species are toxigenic, meaning they can produce toxins.

How exactly these mycotoxins (toxins produced by mold or other fungi) affect people is still somewhat of a mystery. Some experts have concluded that mycotoxins have been responsible for mucous membrane irritation, skin rash, nausea, immune system suppression, acute or chronic liver damage, acute or chronic central nervous system damage, endocrine effects, and cancer. But others claim that the research isn't enough to confirm that these ailments were caused by mycotoxins.

So is "toxic mold" a concern? The United States Environmental Protection Agency (EPA) advises:

> **"More studies are needed to get a clear picture of the health effects related to most mycotoxins. However, it is clearly prudent to avoid exposure to molds and mycotoxins."** [i]

Allergies and Asthma

Exposure to mold can cause any of the symptoms associated with other environmental allergies: runny nose, sneezing, nasal congestion, watery eyes, or skin irritation. Mold exposure can also spur attacks in asthmatic individuals, and a recent study indicated that the odds of developing asthma were more than two-fold if a child lived in a home with high mold levels during infancy.[ii]

As with any allergic reaction, the severity of the reaction can vary. Just as one person can be allergic to cats while everyone else in the house enjoys the family pets, there may be only a single family member made miserable by an indoor mold problem. We have even had clients who reported no problems at all, but a close friend or member of the extended family has an allergy or asthma attack each time they visit.

Fungal Infection

Although not as common as allergic symptoms or even those thought to have been brought on by mycotoxin exposure, some individuals can develop fungal infections where fungus actually starts to colonize on or in the body. This type of infection generally affects the lungs, sinuses, or skin. But with the exception of some common skin infections (e.g., "athlete's foot" can be caused by a type of mold), fungal infections do not normally affect otherwise healthy individuals. They are sometimes referred to as "opportunistic infections," because they rarely occur in individuals who do not already have a compromised immune system.

Mold Remediation 101

Clearly it's important to clean up indoor mold problems, to

GIVING YOUR CUSTOMERS THE ROYAL TREATMENT

protect your home or place of business and those people close to you. But what exactly does that mean? Can't you simply spray some bleach on the contaminated area and kill the mold? The short answer is "No."

Removal is the Key

Although killing the mold may stop the spread of structural damage in your home, it most likely will not be enough to keep your family healthy. Consider someone you know with an allergy to dogs. Would you be surprised if he or she had an allergic reaction when walking into a house where dogs lived, even if the dogs weren't there at the time? Of course not! The allergy is often associated with the hair or dander. Then why is it surprising that dead mold can cause health issues? In fact, the EPA says it best:

> "The purpose of mold remediation is to remove the mold to prevent human exposure and damage to building materials and furnishings. It is necessary to clean up mold contamination, not just to kill the mold. Dead mold is still allergenic, and some dead molds are potentially toxic."[i]

What is the best way to remove mold? That depends on the surface it is growing on. Mold remediators use a variety of methods: HEPA vacuuming, sanding, brushing, scrubbing, wet wiping (*not* just spraying something on the mold), or even blasting with a medium such as dry ice, soda, glass beads, or walnut shells.

Unfortunately, not all companies that claim to remediate mold are actually removing it. Some companies claim that the mold simply needs to be "encapsulated" by applying an anti-microbial coating over the mold. Anti-microbial coatings are fine for helping prevent future mold in areas that have a tendency to become moist, but they should never be applied *over* the mold.

Beware of Bleach

Other companies confuse mold removal with stain removal. It's a common misconception that when the mold stains are no longer visible, the mold is gone. Some companies take advantage of this misconception by simply spraying on stain removal products instead of removing the mold. The "treated" area may look great, and the product may even kill the mold, but unless removed dead mold can still present health risks. Why would a company do this? Because doing the job right can be time consuming and expensive. Spraying on a stain remover which often contains sodium hypochlorite (bleach) is quick and easy, but not the right thing to do.

Another misconception is that the mold isn't gone until all of the stains are removed. This is far from the truth. The Institute of Inspection Cleaning and Restoration Certification, publishers of the accepted industry standards for mold remediation specifically state that stains do not indicate contamination, and that the purpose of stain removal is only to enhance appearance.[iii] A qualified mold remediator knows that stain removers have their place, but it's primarily cosmetic.

Alternative Treatments

Through the years, we've seen some interesting proposals for treating mold contaminated buildings without removing the mold: fogging chemicals, ozone treatment, and ultraviolet lights. None of these methods can replace professional removal, and some can actually be dangerous to the people living in the home. We always remind our customers: If it seems too good to be true, it probably is.

GIVING YOUR CUSTOMERS THE ROYAL TREATMENT

Can't I Do It Myself?

I've already admitted that professional mold remediation isn't cheap. Why would someone hire my company instead of removing the mold themselves?

Trying to do it yourself can cause more harm than good. Remember how mold reproduces? Microscopic spores easily travel through the air. Remember the dandelion? Imagine grabbing a handful of those white puffballs and shaking them. That's what can happen when a homeowner attempts to clean up mold contaminated materials. In fact, over the years we have been hired to perform several remediations after homeowners or unqualified contractors have made the problem significantly worse.

A professional mold remediation technician understands these risks, and takes several precautions to limit cross contamination. In fact, much of the cost of mold remediation is related to these precautions. Before a project is even begun, we set up a containment system around the work area and install air scrubbers. If possible, we create a negative pressure system so the airborne spores are literally sucked out of the home.

The Role of an Indoor Environmental Professional

With very few exceptions, we almost always recommend that potential customers consult with an Indoor Environmental Professional, or "IEP." I've often been asked by others in the business why our company would make this recommendation. After all, the customer has already contacted us. Everyone at my company has received extensive training and has the ability to develop a quality mold remediation plan for most projects. Why add this possible complication that might mean we don't get the job?

Unfortunately, the mold remediation industry has a bad rap. I have read numerous articles and watched too many news programs documenting how unscrupulous companies claimed that extensive remediation work was warranted when there wasn't even a problem. An IEP's job is to thoroughly evaluate the situation, make recommendations for corrections of the underlying moisture problem, develop a remediation plan (if necessary), and do post-remediation verification (if appropriate). If there isn't a problem, the IEP will say so. The IEP acts as an unbiased third party, and has nothing to gain by inventing issues or blowing a situation out of proportion.

An IEP's remediation plan also helps homeowners compare estimates from remediation companies. It states the necessary steps to solve the problem, so all companies are bidding on the same work. And if the homeowner wants to feel confident that the mold was successfully remediated, an IEP can provide that verification. Some companies will provide their own post remediation testing, but accepted industry standards clearly state that an unbiased third party is preferable. [i]

Hiring the Right Mold Remediator

Finding out that there is mold on your property can be a stressful situation, with one of the biggest stressors being finding the right company to do the job. Although it's tempting to want everything fixed quickly, make sure you take time to do your research. We recommend that you consider the following tips when selecting a contractor:

- Review a company's certifications, but remember that not all certifications are the same. We

recommend companies that obtain certification through the Institute of Inspection, Cleaning, and Restoration Certification (IICRC.org), American Council for Accredited Certification (ACAC.org), or Restoration Industry Association (RestorationIndustry.org).
- Ask about using an IEP. If a company seems opposed to using a third party, ask why.
- Verify that the company is properly insured by requesting a Certificate of Insurance.
- Investigate the company's records with the Better Business Bureau or consumer review websites, such as Angie's List™.
- Review the estimate carefully, and don't be afraid to ask questions. If a company proposes to do something other than *remove* the mold, move on.
- Don't make your decision on price alone. You may wind up paying more in the long run if you try to cut corners. My company's bid is rarely the least expensive, because we refuse to cut corners.
- Make sure that the warranty covers labor, as well as materials. Many companies simply pass along the warranty for the antimicrobial coating they use. You will still need to pay for labor if something goes wrong.
- Shop around for reconstruction. If drywall or other materials need to be removed, you can often save money by having a third party replace them once the mold remediation is completed. It doesn't make sense to pay highly trained mold remediation technicians to do something that could be done by a carpenter or handyman.

These tips should help get you on the right path of finding an excellent mold remediation company. Rectifying the situation right the first time, in a safe and efficient manner, and at a fair price should be your ultimate goal.

---

i. *A Guide for Mold Remediation in Schools and Commercial Buildings,* US Environmental Protection Agency, 2001

ii. Reponen T, Vesper S, Levin L, Johansson E, Ryan P, Burkle J, Grinshpun SA, Zheng S, Bernstein DI, Lockey J, Villareal M, Khurana Hershey GK, Lemasters G. 2011. High environmental relative moldiness index during infancy as a predictor of asthma at 7 years of age. Ann Allergy Asthma Immunol 107(2):120-126.

iii Institute of Inspection, Cleaning, and Restoration Certification (IICRC): *IICRC S520 Standard and Reference Guide for Professional Mold Remediation.* 2008. Vancouver, Wash.

GIVING YOUR CUSTOMERS THE ROYAL TREATMENT

About Greg Bowen

Greg Bowen is the Founder and CEO of Alliance Restoration, Inc., Northwest Chicago's premier mold, water, and fire solution. Greg holds CMRS (Council-Certified Mold Remediation Supervisor), ASD (Applied Structural Drying Technician), and WRT (Water Damage Restoration Technician) designations and has spent several thousand hours overseeing the cleanup of homes, offices, and commercial buildings damaged by mold over the past fifteen years.

As a loving husband and father of twins, Greg understands that his customers' concerns run the gamut from "Can I afford this?" and "Will I ever be able to sell my house?" to "What can I do to keep my family safe?" He has built his business on the premise that a company offering mold removal services has a responsibility not only to provide quality service, but to take the time to educate customers and develop a plan that meets their individual needs.

As a result of his focus on education and the willingness to speak frankly about mold, he is often asked to speak as an expert to chamber groups, real estate professionals, property managers, and homeowners associations. Greg is also well-known for his ability to deal with complex situations, especially those where another company's efforts have failed to resolve or even exacerbated the problem.

To speak more with Greg about how Alliance Restoration can help you, contact him at **GBowen@ARICanHelp.com**

Bonus Offer

Got Mold?

For a *Free*

Homeowner Moisture Assessment Checklist

contact us today at

GBowen@Aricanhelp.com

GIVING YOUR CUSTOMERS THE ROYAL TREATMENT

"THANKS TO CHRISTINE HOWATT, I REALLY STAND OUT FROM ALL OF MY COMPETITION!"

Chapter 14

4 Simple Strategies That Will Make Your Business Stand Out From the Crowd (or from your Competition)

By Christine Howatt

There are so many strategies, techniques, and actions an entrepreneur can take to make his or her business stand out and succeed wildly, or fail miserably. Yes, one can do a whole bunch of wrong things under the guise of being busy, following outdated rules, or just doing what everyone else is doing and end up losing money, closing up shop and wondering what the heck happened!

The smart entrepreneur will take massive action with strategies that may seem crazy, abnormal, or counterintuitive; in other words, they're not following the crowd, and see much success.

Over the past few years I've been a student of learning how to succeed in business. I started what I thought was a strictly online business, but I've learned that I have to do more than just sit at my computer and wait for customers to find me on the web. I've read many books, attended seminars, joined business groups to be around successful people, and joined a coaching group, which turns out to be one of the most helpful things I've done.

So here are a few of my favorite strategies, in no particular order, which will make your business stand out and give you an edge over your competition.

GIVING YOUR CUSTOMERS THE ROYAL TREATMENT

1. **Tell a story.** People love stories. They make you more interesting, they can teach without lecturing, they can sell when you can't. So I'll tell you my story. Why did I start a business to sell non-lethal self-defense products? Fortunately, I've never been a victim of a violent crime. I've never taken a martial arts class. I've never been in the military or in law enforcement. I'm just an average woman living an average life. The only thing that ever happened to me is that when I was in college, my purse was cut open and my wallet stolen while riding the subway. But I wasn't hurt. I grew up in a very safe neighborhood in a large city, but I was always aware of my surroundings, carried my keys between my fingers, kept away from dark areas, and did many of the things many young women are taught to do to protect themselves.

Then, about five years ago, I attended a work seminar about personal safety and I purchased some pepper spray for my keychain, along with a larger canister for home. I kept the large canister on my dresser next to my bed and I've carried the smaller pepper spray on my keychain ever since. And yes, I am fully prepared to use them.

I was always on the look-out to start some type of business and came across the chance to sell self-defense products. Since I already carried pepper spray, I thought it would be a good idea. Many business gurus will tell you to have a burning passion for what you do. Did I have a passion for selling self-defense products? Well, no. Frankly, the idea of selling pepper spray, stun guns, hidden cameras, and other weapons just seemed to be kind of cool! But the more I learned about the products and about crime statistics in our country, I also thought I could encourage others, especially women, to take their safety seriously. Crime is everywhere, whether you live in an urban or rural area, and everyone can be a victim, regardless of gender or age.

I know that no one wants to think about the possibility that their daughter, who is away at college, might be raped, or that a team of burglars has been watching their house for a few days waiting for the right time to break in, or that the live-in nanny is smacking the newborn when he cries. Yet when something does happen, they appear totally surprised that such a thing could happen to them.

So hopefully, by telling stories about people I know or about people in the news that have been victims or who had a scary encounter, I can help educate and protect people by making them aware of situations and how to make sure those things don't happen to them.

2. **Relationships with your customers**. After getting the first customer, the new entrepreneur will jump for joy. Woo-Hoo! Now what? Most average business owners will just count their money and wait for the next "sucker," not realizing the value of their existing customers. How do you treat that customer after the sale? You may be thinking that this doesn't matter, the customer is gone and you've got their money. Think about this—do you sell something that person needs again? Does that person have family and friends who may need what you sell? Does that person belong to any groups or have influence in your area and may spread the word about your company or products? That

customer probably has more value than just the first dollar they gave you. Think about how many times that customer may buy from you over a period of years, and what that may be worth to you in real dollars. When I sell a pepper spray to a customer, hopefully she will never have to use it, but she may be happy with her experience with my company and tell her friends about me. Or she may decide to purchase a personal alarm or a stun gun for her daughter. If I just forget about her, she'll most likely forget about where she bought her pepper spray, knowing it was just some place online. She'll just buy from someone else.

You need to set up some type of ongoing communication with your customers. This could be many things. For example, a thank you note after the sale, an offer to buy another product, perhaps at a discount, weekly emails, a monthly newsletter, semi-annual sale notices, an invitation to an event or webinar you're holding, etc. Don't let them forget about you. An existing customer is valuable, and also costs you less than going out to find a new one. Make them your friend and treat them as such.

3. **Offer great value.** What does this mean? Remember the saying "Under-Promise and Over-Deliver?" At a time when anyone can go online, search for an item, click on the first business they see to buy that item, check out the price and then buy, it's very difficult to stand out and show how you're better than the others. In your marketing and advertising, whether online or offline, you have to show that you're the better choice. Since, believe it or not, not all people shop on price, what else can you give that customer that will make them feel like they got

their money's worth and more? Again, this will depend on your business, but can you offer them a 90-day money back guarantee, a free e-book, 30-day free access to a members-only site, coupon for a local business that you've set up a partnership with, a free consultation for a family member, multiple ways to order, or upgraded Priority shipping? These things don't have to cost a lot of money, but their perceived value may be great. Some of the things I offer are a special report for opting in on my website, a 60-day guarantee on most products, and free shipping over $100.

A greater perceived value before, during, or after the sale will make your business the obvious choice. This, along with strategy #2, relationships with your customers, will go a long way to putting you on the path to success. Make sure your customer is so overwhelmed with the value they're getting from you that the actual price of the item is no longer an issue. Depending on your product or service offered, this could mean a lot to your business' bottom line.

4. **Become the Expert**. But all those other businesses are better than me, but I'm just starting out, but I just sell a few things part-time, but I'm not smart enough, but I don't like public speaking, but, but, but...just a bunch of whiny excuses. Sometimes all you need to know is a little bit more than your customers. If I know how to recharge a stun gun, I know more than my customer who never even touched one. If I write a simple report about some basic self-defense tips that I learned from interviewing a local policewoman, I may know more than the single

mom of three kids who's working two jobs and doesn't have time to think about her own safety.

Become the authority figure or expert in your customers' eyes by writing a monthly newsletter, writing articles or a book, posting to your blog regularly, having live demonstrations in your store, starting a club with guest speakers, finding groups to speak to about your products and company, writing a column in the local newspaper, having your picture taken with celebrities that you meet at a seminar or event, or getting interviewed on radio or local cable TV station. If you don't like to write, hire a ghostwriter to do it. If you don't like public speaking, have one of your employees who loves to do that stuff represent you and your company. If you're shy, step out of your comfort zone, take a baby step and do something small to start. Your confidence will rise and you'll be able to do more. Study your own products and know more about them than anyone else. You should know about new developments or research coming to the marketplace that may affect your business.

It's not too hard to become the "expert." Just keep a step ahead of your customers, along with letting them know that you're the expert, the "go-to" person for advice, education, training and/or products.

It takes time to build a business. Any overnight success you've seen usually has had countless years of behind-the-scenes activity.

The successful entrepreneur needs to take steps every day to market his or her business. He or she can't just think about it, wish the economy was better, hope for more customers, wait for a holiday season to pump up sales, or keep going to seminars without putting any of those great ideas into action.

I sincerely hope these four strategies above will give your business a boost to stand out from the competition, give you happy, valuable customers, and give you the business of your dreams!

GIVING YOUR CUSTOMERS THE ROYAL TREATMENT

About Christine Howatt

Christine Howatt is the president and founder of Platinum Security Products, providing "Peace of Mind in a Crazy World." She helps people feel safer and more secure at home, work, and play by offering non-lethal self-defense and security products.

Educating people through her blogs and articles, Christine explains the types of self-defense products on the market, their purpose, and their effects. This enables her readers to become better informed when they are ready to purchase self-defense products. Armed with this knowledge, the average person can truly see themselves as having the ability to defend themselves and their family.

Christine is a successful entrepreneur with several years of marketing and Internet marketing experience, along with many years of experience in the financial/accounting and real estate fields. She wants to instill awareness without paranoia about crime and self-defense.

Christine resides in northern Illinois with her husband and two sons. When she's not out trying to save the world, she enjoys crocheting, bike riding, baking, gardening, traveling, and

CHRISTINE HOWATT

exercising her 2nd amendment rights.

For information on how you can start feeling safer today, or to learn about the products and how to use them, connect with Christine at **www.PlatinumSecurityProducts.com** or directly at **312-344-3667**.

Bonus Offer

15% off

Any Order

with coupon code

"BOOK15"

www.PlatinumSecurityProducts.com

GIVING YOUR CUSTOMERS THE ROYAL TREATMENT

"THANKS FOR THE GREAT ADVICE, PHIL BRAKEFIELD!"

Chapter 15

WINNERS!

Hardware Store Promotional Products that WORK!

By Phil Brakefield

Over the past forty years of service to the independent hardware store industry, we've seen lots of stores have great success in using promotional products as a vital part of their marketing mix.

Some programs have been "one and done promotions," while many others have taken on a "continuity based" approach.

Below are some proven winners that don't break the bank, but do establish strong brand identity in your customers' eyes.

For Contractor Customers:

Tape measures, food gifts (especially during the Christmas season), fluorescent carpenter's pencils, insulated lunch totes, stainless and double-walled travel mugs, caps, jackets, tool totes with speakers, cell phone holders, can coolers, mugs and hard hats.

For Lawn and Garden Customers:

Rain gauges, garden clogs, soft handle gardening tools, garden tool totes, watering cans, aprons, sun bonnets, kneeling pads, watering globe stakes, spray bottles, low flow hose nozzles, gardening gloves, Old Farmer's Almanacs, cell phone holders and seed/bulb packets. There are also small gift-size plants that can be given that will reside in the recipient's home, office or kitchen.

GIVING YOUR CUSTOMERS THE ROYAL TREATMENT

For Painters and Paint Customers:

Painter's caps, paint paddles, shop aprons, painter shape stress reliever, painting guides, home improvement kits, bib overalls, paint can opening tools, drip guards, sweatshirts and tee shirts, insulated lunch totes, business cards with appointment setting copy on the back of the card, cell phone holders and double-wall insulated mugs.

For Employees:

Service award pins, shirts, vests, cell phone holders, food gifts, plaques, trophies, umbrellas and personal planners.

For "Regular" Customers:

Pens, pencils, yardsticks, chip clips, caps, t-shirts, hoodies, walking sticks, lip balm, "how to" guides, shopping bags, portfolios, notepads, Frisbees, water bottles, mugs, flags, lapel pins, balsa wood gliders, coloring books (for the kids), key chains, refrigerator magnets, flash lights, highlighters, mini-tool kits and calendars.

Obviously, there are many of the items listed above that will work for all the categories shown, as well as many other categories not included in this listing.

The Best Bang For Your Buck????

If I had to pick the ONE single item that I think represents the ultimate best value for your promotional product budget, and which is an ideal fit for any customer category imaginable, I would pick as the hands down winner....

Calendars

Calendars are very cost-effective.

Calendars are available in styles that are in keeping with your market area.

And...you can get some great ones for under $1.00!

Even in this day of tablets, iPhones, Androids and all manner of technology driven media, a calendar hanging on the wall of a home or office is looked at between two and ten times EVERY DAY!

If we make a conservative estimate that a calendar, with your name, address, phone, website and logo is seen by your customer only six times a day, that means over the course of a year you get 2,190 marketing impressions, directed EXCLUSIVELY to your ideal customer!

A little more math reveals that if the calendar, with all the power of your imprinted contact information, costs you $1.00, then the CPI (Cost Per Impression) is only about .00045 cents!

In my 40 years of experience, there is no greater marketing tool for a hardware store than a robust calendar program. Nothing else even comes close!

Many stores now want their calendars delivered as early as the beginning of September in anticipation of their customers who come in asking when the next year's calendars are going to be available and what the theme will be.

TRY THESE ON FOR SIZE IN YOUR STORE...WE _KNOW_ THEY WORK!

Over the past 40 years we have been serving the market. Here are some pictures of proven, perennially popular and top-performing promotional products hardware stores have used to great benefit.

GIVING YOUR CUSTOMERS THE ROYAL TREATMENT

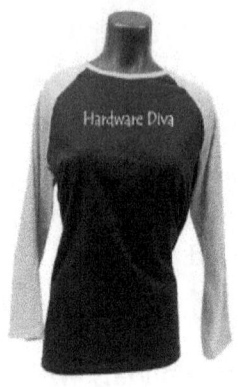

The true, original HARDWARE DIVA design!

Many stores have outfitted their cashiers and other staff in these fun shirts...and many stores have had such a positive reaction from their customers that they are now retailing the HARDWARE DIVA line!

Other designs available include PAINT DIVA, GARDEN DIVA, PLUMBING DIVA and HOUSE WARES DIVA.

The DIVA graphic can be applied to t-shirts, baseball shirts (pictured), sweats, hoodies and caps! Or any other apparel item you choose.

Lunch bags, insulated can carriers, cinch bags, back packs and bags of almost any type are enormously useful to your customers and give you really large real estate to imprint and keep your logo and name front and center.

If you consider using bags, we find that male customers especially enjoy receiving just about anything that features a camouflage pattern.

Insulated travel mugs, water bottles, ceramic mugs and drink ware of just about any genre are HUGE categories for hardware stores to take advantage of when choosing promotional products.

If you choose coffee mugs, you can add a lot of extra perceived value by adding a tea or coffee packet imprinted with your logo and store contact information. For extra special customers, you can then send them a card along with a tea or coffee packet every month to thank them for their business. NONE of your competitors will be doing this, and your customer will be blown away by the gesture. And not only will they continue to shop with you, they will give you tons of referrals.

For most hardware stores, Lawn and Garden is a significant department that delivers a lot of dollars to the bottom line.

Everyone from landscape contractors to home hobbyists are potential customers in this important category, and the selection of promotional products to support that department is strong and wide. Whether you choose anything from rain gauges to wind chimes, an imprinted promotional product with a gardening theme will keep your name in front of your customers' eyes while they are doing what they love most!

GIVING YOUR CUSTOMERS THE ROYAL TREATMENT

It's hard to beat the value of giving your customers a wall calendar every year! You will find that they will start asking when the new ones will be available...so much so that a lot of stores now want their calendars delivered in early September!

Calendars also make a great mailing/marketing piece you can use to re-establish contact with customers you haven't seen in a while, or send one out to prospects along with a letter inviting them to visit your store. Include a gift certificate in that mailer, and watch the new footsteps head your way!

AND DON'T FORGET THERE ARE LITERALLY HUNDREDS OF THOUSANDS OF PROMOTIONAL PRODUCTS TO CHOOSE FROM, AND THERE ARE THOUSANDS THAT ARE PERFECTLY SUITED TO YOUR BUSINESS!

PHIL BRAKEFIELD

Thank You for your interest in this book...

My hope is that you have gotten some strategies and tactics you can tweak a bit and use in your own business, and most especially, that you now understand the incredible power that a carefully selected assortment of promotional products can have on customer retention, referrals, and most importantly, on your bottom line!

In appreciation for your purchase of this book, please accept the GIFT CERTIFICATE below to be used on any future purchase from UniSource. **(I want to make this book FREE for you!)**

Let's keep it simple!

Bonus # 1

Redeem this certificate for

20% off
any purchase over $100!

www.Unisource-Promos-Club.com

GIVING YOUR CUSTOMERS THE ROYAL TREATMENT

Bonus # 2
($250 Value)

FREE
15 Minute Consultation

Phil@Unisource-Promos-Club.com

Phone: (800) 859-2831

Further Reading and Study

Did you enjoy reading about how these sharp entrepreneurs have used each of these strategies to grow their businesses?

Do you think you could make any of these strategies work for you and your business?

All of the strategies in this book – and many more – are explained and taught step-by-step at SSSMarketingUniversity.com.

That site has been called
"The Single Most Dynamic Client Attraction Program Ever Created"

You can take advantage of a 30-Day Free Trial as a Bonus for reading this book by going to:

www.SSSMarketingUniversity.com/bookbonus

www.ingramcontent.com/pod-product-compliance
Lightning Source LLC
Chambersburg PA
CBHW051654170526
45167CB00001B/463